COLORADO'S

# Legendary
# Lovers

*Historic Scandals,
Heartthrobs, and
Haunting Romances*

Rosemary Fetter

Text copyright © 2004 Rosemary Fetter

Library of Congress Cataloging-in-Publication Data

Fetter, Rosemary.
  Colorado's legendary lovers / by Rosemary Fetter.
     p. cm.
  Includes bibliographical references.
  ISBN 1-55591-372-5
  1. Colorado—Biography. 2. Man-woman relations—Colorado.
3. Frontier and pioneer life—Colorado. 4. West (U.S.)—Biography.
5. Couples—Colorado—Biography. I. Title.
  CT226.F48 2005
  920.0788—dc22

                                                    2004022380

Printed in the United States of America
0 9 8 7 6 5 4 3 2 1

*Editorial:* Faith Marcovecchio, Katie Raymond, Haley Groce
*Design:* Patty Maher
*Cover image:* From an antique valentine, c. 1905

Fulcrum Publishing
16100 Table Mountain Parkway, Suite 300
Golden, Colorado 80403
(800) 992-2908 • (303) 277-1623
www.fulcrum-books.com

To my mother, who always told me,
    "You should write a book."

# Table of Contents

### CHAPTER III
### SCANDALS AND TRIANGLES

CHAPTER VI
HAUNTING ROMANCES

# Foreword

*M*any of Rosemary Fetter's fellow Colorado authors, myself included, are probably pounding their desks and keyboards, asking themselves, "Why didn't I think of a book like that?"

This seductive paperback is a terrific way to meet many of Colorado's most memorable characters and the lovers who, more than most biographers will tell you, spurred them to greatness. Rosemary, a Colorado native and seasoned Denver author, shows how these loves shaped Colorado, or at least made headlines. One of the most haunting tales is that of a beautiful Indian woman who married and sustained a Ute chief trying to keep peace. Chipeta and Chief Ouray were inseparable, and she remained his friend and confidante during the Utes' most troubled times. She helped Ouray negotiate peace in the wake of the Meeker Massacre, accompanying him in 1880 to Washington, D.C., where she was proclaimed the "Queen of the Utes." After Ouray died, she spent her last forty-four years in dire poverty, living in a teepee in the Utah desert.

The characters chosen for the book all have compelling stories. Julie Penrose converted Colorado's most extravagant playboy into the state's premier philanthropist, while Hattie Sancomb changed Colorado history with a potshot at errant lover William Newton Byers, ending his editorship of the *Rocky Mountain News* and potential political career. Louise Hill and Bulkeley Wells made adultery fashionable for the upper class. Mary and John Elitch founded a landmark amusement park and theater that entertained Coloradans for generations. Some were saints and others sinners, but they all shaped the highest state.

Many books give you less than you expect from their blurb promises. *Colorado's Legendary Lovers* gives more. Herein look for engaging little sidebars, ranging from "Love Locks: The Art of Hair Jewelry" to "Flowerspeak." The latter instructs lovers to send brambles to show remorse and a striped carnation to terminate a relationship. Striped carnations, of course, are cheaper than divorce attorneys.

Unlike many of her romance-minded predecessors, Rosemary tries to separate fact from fiction in this collection of colorful character profiles. She is an adept researcher who has a gift for popularizing history and bringing characters to life on the printed page. Her honesty, clarity, graceful writing, and wit make this a sweetheart of a book.

This is a book for anyone wanting charming mini-stories of Colorado's movers and shakers and shockers. Here's to you fellow readers and fellow romantics and, as you will discover herein,

> *Here's to those who love us,*
> *If we only cared.*
> *Here's to those we'd love*
> *If we only dared.*

—*Thomas J. Noel*

# Acknowledgments

*T*his book owes a great debt to many historians and writers, whom I hope I have credited sufficiently in the bibliography. I would particularly like to thank my longtime friend and mentor, Dr. Tom Noel of the University of Colorado at Denver, whose lively Colorado history classes inspired my further research into the secret lives of the formerly famous. (As Noel once put it, "I prefer to write about the dead. They don't contradict you.") Other Colorado historians and colleagues who were particularly supportive and helpful include my friends Cathleen Norman and Bonnie McCune. Peg Eckstrand, Betty Lynne Hull, Sylvia Pettem, Linda Jones, Jan MacKell, Deborah Dix, Julie Kanellos, Stan Oliner and Modupe Labode, chief historian at the Colorado Historical Society, all provided vital information and suggestions, as did Marianne Glacer, daughter of Bulkeley Wells.

Research librarians are invaluable to any writer, and I would like to thank the Denver Public Library Western History Department staff, particularly Colleen Nunn and Bruce Hanson. Marshall Edson at the Iliff School of Theology Library provided a great deal of assistance, along with the staffs of the Colorado Historical Society's Stephen H. Hart Library, the Littleton History Museum, the Kit Carson

Museum, and the Golda Meir Museum. The Denver Woman's Press Club Critique Group provided an additional nudge that helped me get this project off the ground.

Finally, I would like to thank my longtime pals Sandra Elliott, Kay Hornor, Kate Kienast, and Anne Reynolds and my sons, Mark and Chris, who put up with my whining and provided encouragement when I needed it, which was most of the time.

# Introduction

Colorado's snowcapped peaks and crimson sunsets have always provided an inspiring backdrop for romance. Lovebirds flock to the Rockies year-round to celebrate landmark moments, rekindle passion, or simply enjoy the pleasure of each other's company. Myriad love stories thread through the state's past like a colorful tapestry that brings history to life (and vice versa).

Of all Colorado romances, the saga of silver king Horace Tabor and the stunning Baby Doe is the best known. As an opera, a movie, and the subject of innumerable books and articles, the Tabor tragedy has become the quintessential American rags-to-riches-to-rags epic. Perhaps no other state can boast a love story so well publicized.

Although *Colorado's Legendary Lovers* includes the infamous Tabor triangle, I've tried to provide a more balanced view of the state's romantic peaks and valleys. Historic characters such as Margaret Brown (the Unsinkable Molly), Kit Carson, and even Golda Meir should be familiar to readers, but this book examines their actions and contributions specifically in terms of the emotional bonds that shaped their lives. Several stories aim to touch the heart, while others tickle the funny bone, and a few present a surprise or two. Some tales may seem bizarre (or at least curious) and raise questions that may never be answered. Still others reflect a cynicism that is not the exclusive province of the twenty-first century. The majority, however, stubbornly maintain that love really does conquer all, at least some of the time.

The book also attempts to examine the differences between male-female relationships in nineteenth- and early twentieth-century Colorado versus the eastern United States. The fluid nature of the westward movement allowed women new freedom, especially in farming and ranching communities, where the sexes worked closely together for a common goal. As a result, western men were more supportive (or at least more accepting) of expanded roles for women. In 1893, Colorado became the first state where men actually voted in favor of woman's suffrage, twenty-seven years earlier than the rest of the country.

Business and professional opportunities were also better for women. Singer-saleswoman Elizabeth Iliff Warren, for example, relocated to Colorado because of a promotion. Still, Victorian restraints made the combination of career, husband, and family particularly tricky. Most successful professional women remained single, but some went into business with their husbands, including Mary Elitch and Katrina Murat. Others simply took a helpful lover, as did Mollie O'Bryan, the only woman ever to hold a seat on the Cripple Creek Stock Exchange. A few, such as University of Colorado professor Mary Rippon, had to hide their families from the world to keep their jobs.

In general, the time frame of *Colorado's Legendary Lovers* encompasses a period between the early Victorian era (the mid-1840s) and pre-*Titanic* years of the twentieth century (about 1912). Since some characters were long lived, a few segments spill over several decades. I tried not to venture far beyond World War I, which was a watershed event that brought about revolutionary changes in male-female relationships. Although many stories take place along the Front Range, the book reflects the entire Colorado landscape, from the grasslands of the eastern plains to the mountain towns and mining camps. At one point I ventured out of state to compare the fate of Baby Doe Tabor with California's Arabella Huntington, a digression which I hope purists will indulge. I love the story and believe there must be a lesson in there somewhere.

In deference to my readers, who deserve at least a stab at the truth, I've made every attempt to maintain historical accuracy. Diaries or journals are quoted whenever possible to give a firsthand account of events. The text contains no undocumented conversations or musings, since the author was not present and cannot read the minds of the deceased.

In keeping with the title, *Colorado's <u>Legendary</u> Lovers*, I tried to select couples whose lives impacted the state's evolution. I looked for stories that contain an element of drama and reflect the optimism that still characterizes the West. Those chosen were either representative of their era, including pioneers Mollie Dorsey and Byron Sanford, or played specific roles in the frontier landscape, such as Chipeta and Chief Ouray. Gamblers and shady ladies like Cort Thompson and Mattie Silks were inevitable in any western boomtown and provided some intriguing material. Due to space constraints, some omissions were inevitable, but a few juicy tales have been squirreled away for a possible sequel.

The final chapter, "Haunting Romances," examines the plight of Colorado's favorite lovelorn ghosts. The book also contains shorter cameos that focus on individuals rather than couples, such as Colorado's first romance novelist, Cripple Creek real estate baron Verner Z. Reed. Other vignettes take a peek at Victorian customs and curiosities in matters of the heart. These include fashion trends, which rose to heights of absurdity in the nineteenth century and put current fads in perspective.

Like romantic love in general, this book should be experienced mostly for fun. So pull up a comfy chair, pour yourself a glass of wine or a cup of cocoa, put your feet up, and enjoy the sweet and spicy side of Colorado history. You might also keep a box of tissues handy, just in case.

CHAPTER I

# *Natives and Pioneers*

### ❧

## Honeymoon
## on the Santa Fe Trail

*Susan and Samuel Magoffin*

*I*n June 1846, a nineteen-year-old bride with a taste for
adventure became the first American woman to travel the
Old Santa Fe Trail into Mexico. Like many well-educated
young ladies of her time, Susan Shelby Magoffin kept a diary.
With a flair for writing and an eye for detail, she faithfully
recorded her remarkable exploits (along with forty-nine pages
of romantic poetry) for the folks back home in Kentucky.

That year, Santa Fe traders carted more than a million
dollars worth of goods across mountains and deserts into
northern Mexico, a journey of approximately eight or nine
hundred miles, depending on the route. Susan's travels took
place during one of the country's most daring eras, when the
expansionist policies of President James Knox Polk paved the
way for the Mexican War and the subsequent annexation of

Texas, California, and New Mexico, all provinces of Mexico in 1846. Without the blatant prejudice of many observers, Susan provided intriguing insights into the culture of New Mexican inhabitants and the American conquest of Mexico, which nearly doubled the size of the United States.

Susan Shelby was barely eighteen when she married Samuel Magoffin, a veteran Santa Fe trader twenty-seven years her senior. Her family initially opposed the match because of Samuel's age and dangerous occupation, but Susan fell deeply in love with the lanky frontiersman, whom she refers to in her journal as *mi alma* (my soul). Both Susan and Samuel came from tough pioneer stock. Susan's distinguished and wealthy Kentucky kinfolk included Revolutionary War heroes and legendary leaders such as her grandfather, Indian fighter Isaac Shelby. Samuel's folks were Irish immigrants who settled in Kentucky during the 1790s. His family had been involved in the Santa Fe trade since the trail opened up in the early 1820s.

After an eight-month honeymoon in New York, Susan opted to accompany Samuel on a trading venture into Mexico. Magoffin adored his young bride and provided her with every comfort, including a tent house, private carriage, a maid, driver, and two servants. The couple began their journey at Independence, Missouri, traveling across the plains in a honeymoon caravan. She thought herself living "the life of a wandering princess" and wrote, "This is a life I would not exchange for a good deal! There is such independence, so much free, uncontaminated air, which impregnates the mind, the feelings, every thought with purity. I breathe free without that oppression and uneasiness felt in the gossiping circles of a settled home."

Their fifteen-month journey took them through the future states of Kansas, Colorado, and New Mexico and into northern Mexico. They survived wagon breakdowns, near-fatal accidents, dust storms, mosquito infestations, threats of Indian attack, and one of the most exciting periods in American history. Although Susan traveled in relative comfort, the rigorous journey took a heavy toll on her health. Pregnant when she began the journey (although she probably didn't know it), Susan tried to remain cheerful and optimistic, although at one point she admitted, "This business of marriage is not what it is cracked up to be."

After forty-six days of travel, the wagons finally reached Bent's Fort, near Pueblo, Colorado. With rounded, high adobe walls and a single entrance, the fort reminded Susan of an ancient castle. She gives a highly detailed description of the structure, down to its billiard room and makeshift racetrack. "There is no place on earth where man lives and some form of gambling is not carried on," she complained.

She and Samuel soon met up with Gen. Stephen Watts Kearney, who descended upon the fort with a makeshift regular and volunteer army, grandiosely called "The Army of the West." Charged by the government with carrying out a bloodless occupation of New Mexico, Chihuahua, and California, Kearney immediately issued a proclamation annexing much of New Mexico to the United States. Samuel's older brother, James, also joined the couple at the fort.

Gregarious and well liked by the Mexican people, trader James Wiley Magoffin had married into one of Mexico's wealthiest families, and his wife's cousin, Manuel Armijo, served as governor of New Mexico. Magoffin had been selected by President Polk for a secret mission, to use diplomacy and family connections to pave the way for a peaceful conquest of New Mexico. Armed with optimism and a large supply of brandy and claret, the elder Magoffin rode ahead of the army as a goodwill ambassador.

Susan suffered a miscarriage on the day after her nineteenth birthday. Following the loss of her baby she found comfort in religion, as she would many times throughout the journey. During the brief time allowed for her recovery, she noted the behavior of an Indian woman in the room below who had given birth about the same time. "In half an hour she went to the River and bathed herself and it [the child], and this she has continued," Susan wrote. "Some gentleman here told him [Samuel] that he has often seen them [Indian women] immediately after the birth of a child go to the water and *break the ice* to bathe themselves." She later reflected, "It is truly astonishing to see what customs will do. No doubt many ladies in civilized life are ruined by too careful treatments during childbirth."

Susan had a few days to recover before they were forced to leave the fort. Abandoned by the U.S. Army, which had moved ahead, and threatened by both the Mexican Army and the Indians, she cynically reported, " … if danger were near, I should be obliged to buckle on my pistols and turn warrior myself. The doctor thinks I will have to lie down in the carriage, but lest they should need my services I shall be obliged to decline my treatment. There is little romance attached to my life."

As they left the fort and approached the mountains, her outlook and her health improved. Susan often rode or walked ahead of the caravan, which was rambling along at about half a mile an hour through the rough country around Raton Pass. She happily wandered the hills while her pet greyhound, Ring, kept watch for "Indians, bear, panther, wolves, etc." During her jaunts, Susan collected pebbles, shells, wildflowers, or the "quill of a strange bird," clearly describing in her diary the magnificent changing scenery as pinyon trees gave way to pines. Since the primitive road made carriage travel almost impossible, she crossed the pass mostly on foot.

In small New Mexican villages she became the object of fascination for the people with whom Samuel traded. Initially horrified by the children "running about perfectly naked," she prudishly reflected that the women exposed far too much of their arms and necks. Some even used red paint and whitened their faces with flour like "one from the tomb." With a sense of humor she later reported, "I did think the Mexicans were as void of judgment and refinement as the dumb animals until I heard one of them say [about her] 'bonita Muchachita,' [pretty little girl]! I have reason and certainly a good one for changing my opinion. They are certainly a very quick and intelligent people." As her Spanish improved, she began to exchange friendly banter and gossip with the women who came to trade.

When the Magoffins reached Santa Fe, Samuel's brother James greeted them with a supper of champagne and oysters. The charismatic trader had convinced Armijo to surrender the city peacefully, and the New Mexican governor fled to the south as Kearney's army approached. With the Stars and Stripes flying peacefully in the capital city, James immediately moved on to El Paso and his next assignment. In Santa Fe, Susan finally had her own house, dirt floor notwithstanding. She spent her days bargaining at the marketplace and her evenings charming Kearney's young, homesick officers. She even attended a Spanish ball, where she saw the famous Gertrude La Tules, the most famous lady gambler of her time. By October Samuel and Susan were on the road again, worried by gossip from Chihuahua that told of a three-thousand-man Mexican Army marching north to retake New Mexico. To make matters worse, a Mexican and Indian rebellion against the American occupation of Taos resulted in the gruesome death of appointed governor Charles Bent. Rumors also circulated that brother James had been killed by Apaches, although the Magoffins later learned that the Mexicans had taken him prisoner and were treating him well.

Fortunately, Samuel and Susan made it to El Paso without incident. After a pleasant and reassuring stay, they proceeded with the business of trading as the caravan continued to Chihuahua City, Saltillo, Monterrey, and Mier. Susan's moods fluctuated, depending on the stage of her second pregnancy and the reported successes of the American Army. Her journal entries became more sporadic and finally ceased when she and Samuel boarded a steamboat down the Rio Grande del Norte. In Matamoras she suffered a siege of yellow fever that permanently ruined her health. She also gave birth to a son, who only lived a few days. Although her final reflections on the journey would have been enlightening, apparently she lost interest in her diary or became too ill to continue writing.

Upon returning to the United States, the Magoffins settled first in Lexington, Kentucky, then in Missouri, where Susan gave birth to her first daughter. Susan died prematurely at age twenty-eight after the birth of her second daughter. Grief-stricken and despondent, Samuel eventually married her cousin, also named Susan Shelby, who supposedly bore a resemblance to his first wife.

Mexican captors released Samuel's brother James after he provided them with 2,900 bottles of champagne. He later settled at El Paso del Norte, founding what later became the American city of El Paso, Texas.

# LOVE LOCKS:
# THE ART OF HAIR JEWELRY

The mid- to late nineteenth century saw the development of a particularly curious hobby for Victorian ladies. Guided by complicated pattern books, they would spend hours weaving human hair into chains for artwork and jewelry. Although the practice seems ghoulish today, the desire for a physical memento from a friend, lover, or family member can be better understood in light of the high infant mortality rate and short life expectancy of the time (approximately 38.7 years for men and 40.9 years for women). When Queen Victoria's beloved Prince Albert died in 1861, Her Royal Highness wore black for the next forty years, inspiring mourning customs and fashions soon copied in the United States. During the same period, the horrendous casualties suffered during the American Civil War (1861–65) created widows by the tens of thousands. For the bereaved, a piece of jewelry made from the hair of a deceased loved one served multiple purposes: as an accessory, a keepsake, and a grim reminder of life's uncertainties.

Hair jewelry did not always commemorate the dead, and locks of hair were often exchanged between lovers for sentimental purposes. Victorian ladies could create their own hair jewelry or commission artists or "hairworkers," who could personalize the piece with engravings or monograms. Since professionals were notorious for selling custom pieces made from purchased hair rather than the tresses of the beloved, most women chose the "do-it-yourself" method. Ladies first practiced with horsehair, then gathered strands from family members or collected hair from their brushes. The fuzzy treasures were stored in a porcelain or ivory hair keeper on the vanity. After boiling and sorting the locks, women could create pictures and designs using a braiding table and bobbins wound with hair. To complete the work, the braids would be formed into a chain attached to a leaded weight, then dropped through a hole in a table. When completed, the chain could be taken to a jeweler to be finished with gold or brass, or woven into creative artwork. One woman even made an entire hair tea service, which probably sent her guests running for the door.

## 🐾
# Seekers of the Promised Land
*Mollie Dorsey and Byron Sanford*

*A* vivacious brunette with a delightful wit and guileless manner, eighteen-year-old Mollie Dorsey left more than one besotted suitor in the dust when she headed west in 1857. Mollie began keeping a diary as her family emigrated from Indiana to the Nebraska Territory during the country's greatest westward expansion. She would chronicle her activities for the next several years, documenting her romantic escapades along with the adventure and challenges of frontier life. Written with humor and insight, her diary provides a fascinating personal account of the early Nebraska Territory and the birth of Colorado.

In 1854, the Kansas-Nebraska Act opened up a vast area for settlement: all the remaining lands of the Louisiana Purchase in the Nebraska and Kansas Territories, which included Colorado. The act gave every new settler the opportunity to purchase 160 acres from public domain at $1.25 per acre. For landless men like Mollie's father, who had suffered severe business losses during the Panic of 1857, it was the bargain of the century. The Dorseys booked passage on a Missouri riverboat to Nebraska City, where the family settled temporarily. Mollie's father and uncles found a lovely spot in a wooded area next to a stream, not far from the Little Nemaha River. "Father is building a log cabin in the woods. Yes! In the woods! Miles and Miles from anybody!" Mollie whined in true teenage angst. Despite solitude, rattlesnakes, and blizzards, she eventually came to love the land her family called Hazel Dell.

In Nebraska City Mollie attracted more admirers, including a family acquaintance named Cornell. "I have heard he has recently broken an engagement with Miss Pamela Bouleware, who is slowly dying with consumption," Mollie wrote disdainfully. "I am not very well impressed with him." After befriending Pamela, she liked him even less. Knowing that Cornell suffered from painful corns, Mollie discouraged his attentions by dropping her prayer book on his foot during church services. She rebuffed another young man more gently during a fishing trip, when she "accidentally" hooked his hat and tossed it into the water while he was trying to propose.

"I don't know if I will ever love a man well enough to marry him," she wrote despondently. "I so soon tire of gentlemen if they get too sentimental." Mollie would continue to receive proposals before settling down with handsome Byron N. Sanford from Albion, New York. She would spend the next few decades complaining affectionately about his reserved manner.

Thirty-one-year-old Sanford was a direct descendent of Thomas Sanford, who settled in America as a member of England's Winthrop Colony in 1632. A blacksmith and wagon maker, Byron moved to Nebraska City after a fire destroyed his business in Indiana. Mollie called him "the yaller mule driver," because he drove a pair of flesh colored mules, but privately she thought him "the cutest fellow I have ever met."

Byron's dry wit, intelligence, and good looks captivated the previously inaccessible Miss Dorsey. The following passage from her journal, although written in a more innocent age, still has a timeless quality: "We walked along the path admiring the starry heavens and, as I turned to look, he kissed me on the cheek!" Mollie recorded. "It was dreadfully impertinent and I tried to feel offended. He said he knew it was wrong and would take it back, but I kept it to think of, and it burns on my cheek ever since."

Two weeks later she wrote, "I have had a letter, sweet letter. It was not torn to shreds with a wish that he would 'mind his own business,' as some have been fated, but lies securely next to my heart. Byron loves me tenderly, truly, and has asked for my heart in return." After they became engaged, Mollie took a job as a teacher and seamstress in Nebraska City, giving the couple time to become better acquainted. She received yet another proposal, this time from a wealthy man who questioned the long engagement and promised a more affluent lifestyle. With righteous indignation she sent him packing and married Byron in the family kitchen on Valentine's Day 1860.

Two months later, Mollie and Byron caught the second wave of the Pikes Peak gold rush as thousands of emigrants passed through Nebraska City on their way to Colorado. Inspired by a conversation with George West, a Boston newspaperman who later became editor of the *Golden Transcript* newspaper, Mollie convinced Byron that Denver was definitely

Although Mollie Dorsey was not easily impressed, she thought Byron Sanford "the cutest fellow I have ever met." They were married for fifty-four years. *(Courtesy of the Colorado Historical Society, #F-4172)*

"the" place to go. With wagons well stocked with provisions and a few head of cattle, they started out across the Great American Desert with another couple, named Clark. Mollie's younger sister, Dora, and brother-in-law, Sam Harris, went ahead on an earlier wagon train.

The new Mrs. Sanford recorded their seven-hundred-mile trek with diminishing zeal. Averaging twenty miles a day, they found little respite from the burning sun, merciless rainstorms, and monotonous scenery. Mollie lost a prize rooster as they were crossing a river ("Count not your chickens!" she wrote philosophically). She trudged for miles through alkali dust and prickly pears, often preferring to walk rather than ride with the ill-tempered Mrs. Clark.

While driving a small wagon ahead of the group one morning, a terrified Mollie met up with several young Indian braves, who teased her by pretending to slice off one of her braids. Fortunately, her assailants had more interest in her pantry than her body and departed after she gave them sugar and biscuits. On another occasion, an "old buck" offered Sanford several ponies in exchange for his white squaw. Byron politely refused, remarking that, "the poor fellow had never done him any harm." Usually good-natured, Mollie was not amused. "The stern realities are rather taking the jokes out of him and the poetry out of me," she wrote. About two hundred miles out of Denver they encountered disillusioned gold-seekers heading back East. "On one covered wagon I see Pikes Peak or Bust and on one returning, I see Pikes Peak or busted," she mused. "The gold excitement is what takes people there, but we are not expecting much."

Upon reaching Denver, Mollie found her sister and brother-in-law camping on the banks of Cherry Creek. "There are no houses to be had and hundreds of families are living in wagons, tents, and shelters made of carpets and bedding," she observed, estimating that five thousand people were settled around Denver. "It seems so near the mountains that I thought I could walk easily over there, but Dora says they are 12 miles away. The atmosphere is so dry and clear it brings distant objects nearer."

Since Denver already had an abundance of blacksmiths, Byron went to work for Judge Holly, an old acquaintance from Nebraska City who was building a stamp mill near Boulder.

When Byron went out of town on an errand, Mollie took in sewing to keep busy. "The currency here is gold dust or small nuggets ... carried around in small bottles or buckskin bags and weighed out in small scales," she observed. "People don't seem to value money ... I get fabulous prices for sewing."

Appalled by Denver's lawlessness, she felt relieved when Byron took her to Gold Hill, the site of Boulder County's first gold boom. While helping Judge Holly build the stamp mill, Byron learned metallurgy and eventually discovered the first tellurium in the county. Mollie cooked for the crew over a primitive open fire, a grueling task that left her exhausted. Homesick and miserable, she composed romantic poetry about her husband when he was away. "If By were to see this, he would make sport of me, but he never looks in this Journal, I'm sure," she wrote sheepishly. Her spirits rose when they moved to their own cabin and she finally began receiving letters from home.

The possibility of an Indian raid kept the settlement in a state of anxiety. "The news was brought in that the Indians were on the warpath and would probably attack the town," she wrote with a shaky hand in February 1861. "We had arranged that if worse came to worse we [the women] would get in buckets and be let down the mining shafts. I said, 'No, let me die the death of the brave!' I knew that if the women were stored in the bowels of the earth and all the men killed, who would rescue us? I would as soon be scalped as buried alive! After a night of suspense, we were informed it was a hoax. The perpetrator of this joke could not be found, or I think there would have been some hair lost, and not by scalping." She was thrilled when Byron returned from a prospecting expedition for their first anniversary, walking ten miles so they could be together.

Mollie moved to Denver that summer to give birth to their first child, a boy who lived only a few days. With the Civil War looming, Byron accepted an appointment as a second lieutenant of Company H in the Colorado Volunteer Infantry. "The sound of fife and drum is heard morning and night," Mollie wrote on October 10, 1861. "They do not have to drum up the recruits, they come from all quarters … Several of the Gold Hill boys have gone into By's company."

She accompanied Byron when Company H relocated to Fort Wise (later renamed Fort Lyon) about two hundred miles from Denver at the site of Bent's Fort. The Colorado Volunteers were called to action in early March 1862, after the Fourth Texas Confederate Cavalry Regiment invaded New Mexico and threatened Fort Union, a federal post northwest of Santa Fe. Mollie bade her husband good-bye and prepared to return to Camp Weld near Denver. "I felt that I could hardly stand it to be left alone, worse than sick in a strange land, so far away from home, with a swollen face and breaking heart," she wrote. Then she gathered up her courage and rose to the occasion. "I saw the tears trickling down By's face and turned to be the comforter. I heard a voice saying 'Trust in me, I will that ye shall meet again.'"

Lieutenant Sanford distinguished himself at the Battle of Pigeon's Pass, when he and a comrade destroyed an enemy canon and artillery, nearly losing their lives. Led by Col. John Chivington, the Colorado Volunteers defeated the Confederates on March 28, 1862, at the Battle of Glorietta Pass, sometimes called "The Gettysburg of the West." After Byron returned to Fort Weld, Mollie gave birth to another boy, who they named Albert Byron Sanford. Until shortly after their daughter's birth in 1866, Mollie continued to chronicle Denver's triumphs and disasters, including the great Cherry Creek flood and threats of Indian attacks in 1864. "It seems there is one excitement after another, and I wonder that I am not white-headed," she wrote.

After leaving the military, Byron worked for the United States Mint until 1888 and served on the commission that chose the site for the University of Colorado. The Sanfords moved back and forth from Denver to their 160-acre ranch located north of present-day Belleview Avenue and west of Santa Fe Boulevard. The years and hardships never diminished Mollie's sense of humor, her fondness for writing poetry, or her affection for Byron. She wrote the following on their thirty-sixth anniversary:

> By is sick tonight with a very bad cough. I thought I would write him a valentine, but I can show my wifely devotion better by doctoring him. The very thought and urgent need of mustard plasters takes the poetry out of me anyway.

Still, she took a moment to renew her vows with a typically lighthearted verse:

> *With potions then, I'll soothe his pain*
> *And woo him back to health again*
> *It's almost two score years ago*
> *I took him for both meal and woe*
> *And vowed that through both good and ill*
> *I'd be his loving helpmeet, still*
> *I took him for my lord and master*
> *And now I'll go and make that plaster.*

Byron Sanford died on Thanksgiving Day 1914. Mollie followed less than three months later on February 6, 1915.

## VALENTINE SNIPPETS

The lovers' holiday actually began as a spring fertility rite called *Lupercalia*, an annual "coming-of-age" ritual for young Roman males that dates back to the fourth or fifth century B.C. The ancient celebration involved animal sacrifices, imbibing of spirits, half-naked youths chasing after acquiescent maidens, and the usual brouhaha so typical of early Roman festivities. As part of the ritual, the names of eligible girls would be placed in a box and the boys would draw at random to choose a significant other for the forthcoming year.

This hit-or-miss approach to relationships horrified the early Christian church, which often substituted saints' days for pagan celebrations to give the holiday a more acceptable meaning. In a determined effort to snuff out unsanctified teenage sex, the church fathers brought Saint Valentine into the picture. According to legend, Valentine was a Christian priest executed by Emperor Claudius for performing secret marriages among the military. (The emperor disapproved of matrimony on the grounds that it distracted a soldier from the important business of killing, looting, and raping. Also, he had been married to the infamous nympho-maniac Messalina, which may have soured him on women.) At any rate, the good Father Valentine would likely have turned over in his hair shirt had he seen his future place in history beside chubby little cherubs clutching arrow-skewered hearts.

Valentine postcards often got to the heart of the
matter, as shown above. *(Courtesy of the
Rosemary Fetter collection)*

Since old habits die hard, in A.D. 496, Pope Gelasius attempted
to reinvent the lottery by substituting the names of saints for sex
partners. Young people would continue to pick names from a box, but
now they were expected to emulate the life of the saint whose name
they had drawn. For reasons obvious to everyone but Gelasius, this
never worked out. Young Roman males obediently drew their saints'
names and sent clandestine love notes to women they admired.

Somehow the custom of exchanging love messages survived into the Middle Ages. During the late twelfth century, Queen Eleanor of Aquitaine, wife of England's King Henry II, gave romantic love a boost by initiating the Courts of Love, which celebrated chivalry and chaste adoration from afar. Eleanor and Henry never got along too well after that, but hopeless romantic love has been with us ever since. In the fifteenth century, Charles, duke of Orleans, sent the oldest surviving valentine to his wife from the Tower of London, where he was imprisoned.

In 1767, a helpful Englishmen published *The Young Man's Valentine Writer*, containing scores of canned sentiments for the poetically struggling. With the establishment of the penny post in both England and the United States, the custom of exchanging valentines blossomed. Cards ranged from simple woodcut varieties to elaborate artwork decorated with gold or silver leaf, paper or fabric lace, silk flowers, and the ever-popular embossed cupid. Love tokens often went unsigned or signed with initials only, to add to the mystery.

Most inscriptions were cheerful and loving, engraved with simple messages such as, "Accept my heart" or "Yours for eternity." Some were racy and a few positively guilt-inspiring, like this quotation from a penny postcard, circa 1890:

> *Here's to the rose and here's to my heart*
> *They died the selfsame day*
> *Here's to the girl who owned them both*
> *And tossed them both away*

A more encouraging Valentine postcard shows a shy suitor hesitant to pursue his coy ladylove. A masked naked cherub, who holds a pistol rather than a bow and arrow, urges the bespectacled Romeo forward.

> *Here's to those who love us,*
> *If we only cared.*
> *Here's to those we'd love*
> *If we only dared.*

The valentine's popularity peaked around the mid-nineteenth century, about the time gold-seekers began pouring into the isolated mining camp called Denver City. While valentine cards dripping with lace and lofty sentiments whisked across town in eastern cities, Denver's nearest post office was Fort Laramie on the South Platte River. For a quarter apiece, trader Jim Saunders would ride back and forth every thirty days or so delivering letters one- to three-months old. If anyone received a valentine, it probably arrived sometime in April. Service improved with the arrival of the Leavenworth and Pikes stage on May 7, 1859, which brought mail only six days old, much like today's postal service.

The town of Loveland, founded in 1877 by Colorado Central Railroad president William A. Loveland, put Colorado on the map in the romance department. Their post office initiated a program in 1947, so that each Valentine's Day, some 350,000 valentines specially stamped with the "Loveland" postmark are delivered to sweethearts around the world.

### ✿

# The Laughing Maiden of the Utes
*Chipeta and Chief Ouray*

𝒯he five sub-chiefs of the Tabeguache Utes waited nervously at the Los Piños Agency blacksmith shop for the arrival of the legendary Chief Ouray. Wary of his friendship with the white invaders and jealous of Ouray's authority, his subordinates conspired to ambush and murder their leader. The instigator was Sappovonare, brother to Ouray's wife, Chipeta, and his second in command.

An ominous silence descended as Ouray crossed the plaza with Chipeta beside him. As Ouray tied his horse to the hitching post, blacksmith George Hardin gave the chief warning with a nod and a knowing wink. As Ouray entered, Sappovonare sprang from the shop and attacked Ouray with an ax, barely missing his head. Keeping a post between himself and his assailant, Ouray stayed out of range until Sappovonare struck again, this time breaking the ax handle on the post. Overcoming his treacherous in-law, the chief heaved Sappovonare into a ditch. As Ouray reached for a knife to slit his adversary's throat, Chipeta grasped his arm. Speaking quietly, she removed the weapon from his sheath and tucked it into her belt, barely in time to save her brother's life. The four other would-be assassins discreetly disappeared out the back door of the blacksmith shop.

Later, Chipeta mediated a truce between Sappovonare and Ouray. That her brother lived to resume his position as Ouray's commander says much for the chief's patience, but even more about his affection for Chipeta. Ouray's wife was both his friend and confidant. They were practically inseparable from their

Photographer William Henry Jackson described Chipeta as "the most prepossessing Indian woman I ever saw," and added, "Ouray was immensely proud of her." *(Courtesy of the Denver Public Library, Western History Collection, #X-30600)*

marriage in 1859 until the chief's death twenty-one years later. He even took her along on his 1880 diplomatic visit to Washington, D.C., where he made a final attempt to save his people and satisfy the demands of the United States government.

Little is known about Chipeta's background. She may have been a Kiowa Apache, raised by the Utes after her parents died in a raid. With regular and well-defined features, she bore little resemblance to most Ute women, who had flat faces. Statuesque, bright, and exceptionally beautiful, she was called "the Laughing Maiden of the Utes" by white men, although her name has been translated as "White Singing Bird" or sometimes "Spring of Clear Water." Chipeta may have been sister to Black Mare, Ouray's first wife. When Black Mare died, Chipeta cared for Ouray's son, Pahlone, who was still an infant. Chipeta loved children and it broke her heart when the child was lost to them at age five. While Ouray and Pahlone were on a hunting trip, a band of Sioux raiders kidnapped the boy during a surprise raid. Although Ouray and the tribe searched futilely for months, the Sioux had traded the child to the Arapaho, deadly enemy of the Utes. Even though he had no other children, Ouray refused to take another wife when Chipeta remained childless.

Although Chipeta preferred the role of a traditional Ute wife, her husband had become quite an unconventional leader. Ouray's father was a Jicarilla Apache who had been adopted by his mother's tribe, the Tabeguache Utes. Ouray spent his formative years as a sheepherder near Taos, New Mexico, where he learned to speak fluent Spanish and some English. In frequent contact with wealthy white ranchers, he became a keen political

observer. The future leader instinctively understood the futility
of waging war on the whites and knew that the only hopes for
his people lay in negotiation and diplomacy. At eighteen he
returned to the Tabeguache tribe, where his father had become a
chief. Although Ouray observed the traditions of the Plains
Indians, he usually dressed in broadcloth and boots instead of
buckskin and moccasins. His ability to understand the white
man's language made him a natural spokesman and interpreter,
beginning in 1863 when the chief negotiated an agreement
determining the boundaries of the Tabeguache reservation.

Over the years he became a lifelong friend of the Indian
scout Kit Carson. While the tribe was camped near Fort
Garland in 1866, Chipeta became acquainted with Carson's
wife, Josefa, a beautiful and refined Spanish woman. The
couples often dined together, and Chipeta learned the ways
of the whites through Josefa's tutelage. In fact, Carson's wife
served as a role model for Chipeta's defense of Sappovonare.
Chipeta had been present when Josefa prevented her husband
from killing a Ute after the Indian slapped Carson's daughter.
The Carsons' large family may have inspired Ouray and
Chipeta to adopt three children shortly after leaving Fort
Garland. During her lifetime, the "Queen of the Utes" would
take at least ten children under her wing.

As prospectors reported small gold strikes in the San Juan
mountain range, the U.S. government cast greedy eyes upon
Ute land. The Treaty of 1868 ceded nearly a third of Colorado
to the Ute tribes, a vast area from Colorado's southern border
past Pagosa Springs northward as far as present-day Steamboat

Springs, then west to the Utah border. In 1872, a commission from Washington attempted to renegotiate the agreement. When Ouray and other chiefs opposed these efforts, he and eight other members of the tribe went to Washington, D.C., to meet President Ulysses Grant at the White House.

The following year, Ouray reluctantly began negotiations for another treaty with the United States, arranged by Felix Brunot, a Washington commissioner. When Ouray told Brunot about his son's kidnapping ten years earlier, the commissioner promised to search for the boy. Hoping to win favor with the Ute chief and end the long-standing feud with the Arapaho, Brunot finally found Pahlone among the Southern Arapaho, where he had taken the name "Friday." After Ouray and the other chiefs signed the treaty, Brunot brought Ouray and Friday together in Washington. The sixteen-year-old would not accept a Ute chief for a father and returned to the Arapaho. Although Pahlone later considered another meeting with Ouray, the boy fell ill and died before arrangements could be made.

In return for a cash settlement held in trust by the government, the Brunot Treaty of 1873 ceded most of the San Juan country to the United States, but allowed the Utes to hunt on their former land if they did not disturb the settlers. As head chief, Ouray received $1,000 per year as long as he maintained the peace and 160 acres of land, which included a large spring for irrigation, a six-room adobe house, and several other buildings including an outdoor kitchen and corrals. Household furnishings included silver and china, presents to Chipeta during the Washington visits, and a piano, which she never learned to play.

When William Henry Jackson took Chipeta's photo in 1874 for the Hayden expedition, he described the Queen of the Utes as "the most prepossessing Indian woman I ever saw," and added, "Ouray was immensely proud of her." According to a reporter from the *Ouray Times* who visited the Los Piños Agency in 1879, Chipeta was never "the servile thing the other Ute women were. She treated Ouray and all of us as her equals."

Despite the treaty, the Utes refused to leave their ancestral home in the San Juans and became increasingly unfriendly toward white settlers. Hostilities finally erupted in September 1879 when a small band attacked Nathaniel Meeker, the newly appointed Indian agent for the White River bands. A well-respected man with good intentions, Meeker never understood the Utes and placed stringent restrictions on the tribe, plowing up their grazing pastures (and their racetrack) and forcing them to build ditches, barns, and fences. In the face of growing antagonism, Meeker panicked and sent for backup from the U.S. Army. Some members of the tribe retaliated by ambushing the soldiers in a battle that lasted three days and resulted in many casualties. The raiders shoved a stake down Meeker's throat, a grisly commentary on the white man who spoke with a forked tongue.

Although Ouray had been ill, he tried to prevent the attack and later successfully negotiated for release of the captives. Most survivors were the wives and children of the murdered men. According to an account by Flora Ellen Price, whose husband had been a farmer at the agency, Chipeta tenderly cared for the rescued hostages when they were brought to the farm. "We were all treated well at Ouray's house," Flora later testified. "Mrs. Ouray wept for our hardships and her motherly face, dusky and beautiful with compassion, was wet with tears. We left her crying."

On October 30, 1879, the headline in *Harper's Weekly* screamed, "The Utes Must Go!" a sentiment agreed upon by most Coloradans. The following January, Ouray took Chipeta and eleven Ute chiefs to Washington, D.C., to participate in a congressional investigation of the Meeker Massacre. When their train reached South Pueblo, and later Chicago, they were met by violent mobs and threatened with lynching. Chipeta testified along with the others, but the hearings revealed no new information. The only individual ever held accountable was Chief Douglass, who spent a short time at Fort Leavenworth penitentiary. For the U.S. government, identifying Meeker's attackers took second place to removing the Utes from Colorado permanently.

According to a later article in the *Denver Republican*, Chipeta became a celebrity in Washington. "Chipeta was idolized … her raiment was the fancy of the best Eastern dress-makers … she was the rage for the season she was in Washington … Correspondence from the English legation to the court journals called her a 'Mountain Princess' and bespoke for her a hearty reception from the peerage of England should she visit that country, which, at the time, she seriously contemplated." Most of this celebrity occurred only in the minds of Denver journalists. The D.C. press ignored Chipeta except for a few occasions when they noted her presence with Ouray and called her "fat."

On March 6, 1880, Ouray agreed to relocate the tribe to the Uintah Reservation in Utah. Most Ute bands refused to sign the treaty, so the following summer Chipeta and Ouray traveled to the Southern Ute camp to try to gain support. The trip proved too difficult for Ouray. On August 24, 1880, the great chief died of Bright's Disease at Ignacio, Colorado. According to Ute custom, Chipeta, Buckskin Charlie (another Ute leader), and John McCook (Chipeta's brother) buried his body in a secret location.

To validate the treaty, three-fourths of the adult males were required to sign or mark the document. Railroad builder Otto Mears later claimed to have paid $2 apiece for each signature, although many were undoubtedly forged. When formalities concluded, Gen. R. S. Mackenzie, six companies of cavalry, and nine companies of infantry removed all but the Southern Utes, who would be confined to a small reservation in southwestern Colorado. Since Chipeta's land lay on the Colorado side of the state line, she had to move to Utah with her people. Although the government promised the Queen of the Utes an equally large ranch on the reservation, she actually got a two-room shack with no furniture. She soon moved back into a teepee and returned to the Ute way of life, marrying a second time to a White River Ute named Accumooquats in 1883.

In 1916, Commissioner of Indian Affairs Cato Sells made a belated attempt to show appreciation to the woman who had been such a great friend to the whites. In her seventies, Chipeta had been living for years with a small group of nomadic Utes and felt no need for government assistance. As a token, the commissioner presented her with a shawl, and Chipeta gave him a saddle blanket and a picture of herself in return. In a note written with the assistance of the Indian agent, she added, "I am glad there is no more trouble between the Indians and the white people and hope this state of affairs exists through the rest of my life."

Chipeta went totally blind in later years and died of a stomach ailment in 1924. The former Queen of the Utes was laid to rest at Bitter Creek, Utah. The following year, her body was reinterred at Ouray Memorial Park just south of Montrose, the site of her old Colorado farmhouse. An eleven-foot granite tombstone marks her grave. In 1956, the Colorado State Historical Society used the property to build the Ute Indian Museum, which includes Ute artifacts and personal belongings of Ouray and Chipeta. With tribal permission and assistance from John McCook and Buckskin Charlie, Ouray also was reburied in 1925 at the Native American Cemetery at Ignacio.

Many Colorado landmarks recognize Chief Ouray, whose stained-glass portrait hangs in the rotunda of the Colorado State Capitol. A mountain peak, a southern Colorado town, and a memorial also bear his name. Chipeta is recognized in a mural that hangs in the capitol honoring eighteen women integral to Colorado's history and development. In the Black Canyon of the Gunnison River, the beautiful Chipeta Falls is among many place-names dedicated to the kindhearted "Laughing Maiden of the Utes."

### ❧
# The Frontiersman's Bride
*Maria Josefa Jaramillo and Kit Carson*

Notice from the *Columbia Missouri Intelligencer*, October 6, 1826

To Whom It May Concern

That Christopher Carson, a boy about sixteen years old, small of his age, thick set, light hair, ran away from the subscriber living in Franklin, Howard County, Missouri, to whom he had been bound to learn the saddler's trade, on or about the first day of September last. He is supposed to have made his way toward the upper part of the state.

All persons are notified not to harbor, support or subsist said boy, under penalty of the law. One-cent reward will be give to any person who will bring back the said boy.

—David Workman

Kit Carson didn't look much like a hero. One of the most romanticized figures in western history, the legendary scout stood barely five foot, six inches tall. Barrel-chested, freckled, and sunburned, he and had thin reddish brown hair and watchful blue-gray eyes. Born into an impoverished Kentucky family, Carson became apprenticed at fourteen to a saddle maker in Franklin, Missouri, the original starting point of the eight-hundred-mile Santa Fe Trail. Although the boy liked his employer, he felt restless and hungered for "different experiences." He ran away in 1826 to join trader Charles Bent on a caravan headed west.

Bent and his younger brother, William, along with partner Ceran St. Vrain, bought and traded in everything

In 1843, frontier scout Kit Carson married his third and last wife, independent New Mexican beauty Maria Josefa Jaramillo. *(Courtesy of the Denver Public Library, Western History Collection, #B-695)*

from livestock and pack animals to pelts, blankets, buffalo robes, foodstuffs, and manufactured goods. In 1833, the partners built Bent's Fort, which became a bustling trading post on the Arkansas River near present-day La Junta. Carson later worked as a hunter for the Bents, supplying meat for the fort.

Upon arriving in Santa Fe, Kit headed north to Taos, which became his temporary home. After wintering with a retired mountain man, he learned Spanish and became a translator for another trade caravan from Santa Fe to Chihuahua City, Mexico. A successful trapper, tracker, hunter, and later a scout, he had a remarkable gift for languages. Carson may have been illiterate, but along with English and Spanish, he spoke fluent French and eight or more Native American languages. He became a skilled interpreter and negotiator, and a wanderer like the Plains tribes who were both his friends and his enemies. Although he made a better Indian fighter than an Indian agent, no one ever doubted his courage or integrity.

According to army scout Tom Tobin, "Kit wasn't afraid of hell or high water, his private life was clean as a hound's tooth, his word was as sure as the sun's coming up, and he never cussed more'n necessary."

Kit's natural curiosity, memory, and eye for detail made him an excellent scout, a talent not overlooked by explorer John C. Frémont. Between 1842 and 1847, Carson guided Frémont's survey expeditions over the Continental Divide to the Great Salt Lake, the Northwest, and California, opening up a vast territory for American settlement. With the support of the "Pathfinder" and his wife, Jessie Benton Frémont, Kit Carson emerged as a national hero, the quintessential frontiersman celebrated in both newsprint and dime novels.

On February 6, 1843, thirty-three-year-old Kit married Maria Josefa Jaramillo, a remarkably attractive girl who had barely turned fifteen. Although writer Louis H. Gerrard once unkindly characterized her looks as "the haughty, heartbreaking kind," Josefa and her niece Rumalda (three years younger) were the belles of Taos society, noted for their dancing, beauty, and vivaciousness. Josefa had a dark complexion; large, bright eyes; a good figure; and a graceful manner. To win her father's approval, Kit converted to Catholicism in 1842 and promised to wait a year before proposing marriage.

The third Mrs. Carson came from a modestly prosperous family of ranchers and landowners who had settled in the Santa Cruz Valley in 1742. Shortly after her birth in 1828, Josefa's father, Don Francisco Jaramillo, moved the family to Taos. She probably met Carson through her sister, Maria Ignacia Jaramillo, who was Charles Bent's common-law wife and Rumalda's mother.

Kit had been married twice before, both times to Native American women. His first wife, an Arapaho named Waa-nibe, died shortly after the birth of their daughter, Adaline, in 1838. Two years later, Kit's second marriage, to an independent seventeen-year-old Cheyenne named Making-Out-Road, ended when she left him to follow her tribe's migration. Among the Plains Indians, either party easily could dissolve a marriage. A wife simply gave notice by moving the man's personal belongings (along with any children that were not her own) outside the teepee.

Although Kit and Josefa spent months and sometimes years apart, they were deeply devoted. Carson fondly called his young wife "Chipeta," a Spanish nickname for Josefa. While her husband was away, Josefa spent a good deal of time with Ignacia.

During the Mexican War of 1846, Gen. Stephen Watts Kearney appointed Charles Bent civil governor of New Mexico following the American occupation of Taos. When Kearney moved south, a mob of Pueblo Indians and Hispanics led by insurgent Tomasito Romero broke into Bent's home on January 19, 1847. Although Bent tried to reason with the mob, insurgents stormed the house and shot arrows at the governor and his wife. As Ignacia slammed the door shut, a quick-thinking Josefa led Rumalda, Ignacia, and Bent's children to a room adjacent to another adobe house. Using an iron spoon and a poker, the three women opened a hole in the bricks and pushed the children through. They followed, and Bent came last. To the horror of Bent's family, Tomasito captured the wounded governor before he could escape and scalped him alive. The women and children were spared, although the mob later ransacked the Carson home.

After the Mexican War, Carson and his friend Lucien B. Maxwell settled in the Rayado Valley, a ranching and farming supply center fifty miles from Taos. According to writer F. Stanley, Rayado was a crossroads for "Indian agents, merchants, Santa Fe traders, Utes, Jicarillas, outlaws, ranchers, soldiers and Indian scouts." Carson was away most of the time, and Josefa became quite independent, managing a household that eventually came to include six children. She also owned land in the Purgatory Valley, part of the Vigil–St. Vrain land grant that extended into present-day southern Colorado. Interestingly, in the mid-nineteenth century a New Mexican woman enjoyed rights denied to her American counterparts at the time. After marriage, she could keep her own property, wages, and even her maiden name. Josefa showed independence typical of her New Mexican sisters when, on one occasion, she ransomed a four-year-old Apache boy from the Utes by trading Kit's favorite horse for the youngster. Since Carson loved children, hopefully this presented no problem when he returned.

Although he tried to settle down, Kit's restless nature overcame any yearning for domesticity. But he always came back to Taos with shawls, silks, and other fabric for Josefa, who loved to sew. After a sheep drive from New Mexico to California, he presented her with the territory's first sewing machine. Partly because Josefa missed her family, in 1854 Carson transferred his main residence back to Taos and took over the Utah (Ute) Indian Agency. Six years later, he suffered a mishap while leading a party over the San Juan Mountains in southwestern Colorado and was dragged over a precipice, either by a mule or a horse. Although his bruises were superficial, the accident left him with serious internal injuries.

After the outbreak of the Civil War, Carson resigned from the Indian agency to become a lieutenant colonel in the

First New Mexican Volunteer Regiment. He commanded the volunteers in the battle of Val Verde in central New Mexico and fought the Kiowa and the Apache. Most of his military efforts went into the war against the Navajo. Upon their defeat, Carson forced more than eight thousand members of the tribe to make the "Long Walk" from Arizona to Fort Sumner, New Mexico. Still, he professed disgust after the Sand Creek Massacre of 1864, when troops led by Maj. John Chivington attacked a peaceful village of Cheyenne and Arapaho and slaughtered more than two hundred, mostly women and children.

Shortly after his promotion to brigadier general in 1865, Carson took command of troops at Fort Garland in southern Colorado. As his illness progressed, Carson resigned his commission in 1867 and moved the family to the Boggsville settlement. They joined Josefa's niece Rumalda and her husband, Tom Boggs, who were building a ranch on the lower Purgatory River, five miles west of Fort Lyon. Boggs offered Kit and Josefa a temporary home until they could build their own ranch house. At thirty-nine, Josefa still retained some of her former beauty, although a hard life and several children had definitely drained her energy. By this time, the former scout suffered so much pain that he could no longer ride a horse and had to travel by carriage.

In January 1868, Carson became the new superintendent of Indian affairs for the Colorado Territory. Shortly afterward, the government asked him to accompany a Ute delegation to Washington, D.C., where officials hoped to negotiate a treaty that would limit their vast territory. Pregnant with their eighth child (one had died in infancy), Josefa could not have been happy about Kit's departure, although he promised to consult eastern physicians about his deteriorating health.

The Utes signed the treaty on March 2, but Kit's time was short. He told his old friend Jessie Benton Frémont that he had to get home so that Josefa would not hear of his death from a third party. Carson arrived back in Boggsville on April 11, exhausted from the journey and barely able to move. After giving birth to a daughter two days later, Josefa was stricken with childbed fever and passed away on April 23. "Grandfather crawled on his hands and knees to be with her when she died," his grandson later told the *Pueblo Chieftain*. Despondent, Carson followed his beloved a month later on May 23, 1868.

Although Carson's treatment of the Native Americans has been controversial, he played an undeniably important role in the westward movement. One of Colorado's counties bears his name, along with an equestrian statue in Denver, a memorial park in Trinidad, and the Kit Carson Chapel at Fort Lyon.

# The Saga of Mountain Charley
*Elsa Jane Guerin*

*A*ccording to her memoirs, Elsa Jane Guerin began posing as a man to avenge the death of her first husband. She claimed to be the illegitimate daughter of a wealthy Louisiana planter, raised by her bachelor father until he sent her off to boarding school. An early bloomer, Elsa Jane ran off with a Mississippi riverboat pilot named Forest and bore him two children before she turned sixteen. Her contented life as a housewife ended abruptly when she received word that her husband had died in a fight with one of his crew. His killer, a man named Jamieson, had been convicted of the crime but set free on a technicality.

"As my financial condition became more desperate, my desire for revenge increased in inverse proportion," she recorded. "I was bound to visit a terrible reparation but ... I could conceive of no means by which I could reach him [Jamieson]." After exhausting her financial resources, she boldly decided to adopt male clothing and seek employment in areas closed to women. She placed her children with the Sisters of Charity, cut off her hair, and studied the manner-isms of young men. Slightly built, she could easily pass for a teenage boy, and she suffered from an asthmatic condition that left her with a hoarse voice. "I buried my sex in my heart and roughened the surface so the grave would not be discovered," she wrote dramatically.

Elsa Jane got a job as cabin boy on a steamer between Saint Louis and New Orleans, working the river for four years. After a while she began to relish the freedom and the escape from corsets, restrictive clothing, and the inability to see her feet. When she visited her children once a month, however, she wore a dress. Leaving the river in 1854, she began work as a brakeman on the Illinois Central Railroad. While sitting in a hotel lobby one afternoon, she recognized Jamieson and "the blood rushed through my veins as if propelled by electricity … He was not a bad looking man naturally," she observed, "but his appearance was that of one who has all his life yielded to the indulgence of fierce passions." Elsa Jane watched him carefully until after midnight, when he left the hotel and headed toward the river. She followed, made her presence known, and challenged him. Drawing her pistol, she intended to "send his black soul to the devil," but her adversary managed to escape after shooting Elsa Jane in the thigh.

Upon recovery, she gave up the hunt for Jamieson temporarily and headed for California, achieving some success in the mule-freight business. During the Pikes Peak gold rush of 1858–59, she opened a saloon in Denver and began calling herself "Mountain Charley."

While riding outside the city one day, she spotted Jamieson again. Both drew their guns. "I emptied my revolver upon him and should have done the same with its mate had not two hunters at that moment come upon the ground and prevented any further consummation of my designs," she wrote. "Jamieson was not dead and the hunters, constructing a sort of litter, carried him to Denver." Elsa Jane's archenemy recovered from his wounds and revealed the true story, generously absolving her of any blame. Eventually, he left for New Orleans and soon died of yellow fever.

Her thirst for revenge finally appeased, Elsa Jane found that she liked wearing men's clothing and continued operating her Denver saloon during the winter of 1859–60. She gained some measure of fame after journalist Horace Greeley reported her story in a letter to the *New York Tribune*. "Mountain Charley" eventually married her bartender, H. L. Guerin, and sold the saloon. The couple headed for the mountains, opened a boardinghouse, and tried mining for a season. In 1860, Elsa Jane and her husband permanently moved to Saint Joseph, Missouri.

⚘

# Lady Isabella
# and the Mountain Man
### *Isabella Bird and Mountain Jim Nugent*

One of Colorado's unlikeliest love affairs blossomed in the autumn of 1873, when a prim English spinster crossed paths with a one-eyed desperado in the high country of Estes Park. Developing a relationship that went beyond camaraderie, Isabella Bird and Jim Nugent explored the now-popular resort when its primitive wilderness was still "no region for tourists and women." Lady Isabella may have been female, but she could hardly be labeled a typical tourist.

An intrepid traveler, Isabella Bird trekked across continents alone at a time when few Englishwomen ventured far beyond their drawing rooms. The daughter of a Yorkshire clergyman who suffered all her life from severe back pain, she feared that she would become an invalid subject to "the great danger of becoming encrusted with selfishness." Isabella determined to see the world instead. Following the death of her parents, who left enough money to allow her the luxury of travel, she took off for the bush country of Australia at the age of thirty-nine. Petite, plump, dark-haired, with large, luminous gray eyes, Lady Isabella exuded a dignity and natural tranquillity that commanded respect wherever she went. During her travels, she rode

Prim Englishwoman Lady Isabella Bird was
alternately shocked and fascinated by her one-eyed
Estes Park guide, Mountain Jim Nugent. *(Courtesy
of the Tom Noel collection)*

horseback, mules, camels, donkeys, and anything else that
would get her where she wanted to go. Curiously, the back pain
disappeared when she was on the road.

In 1873, Isabella visited Colorado en route from the
Sandwich Islands (Hawaii), intending to climb 14,000–foot
Longs Peak, which had been ascended for the first time only
five years earlier. In Estes Park, she met up with the legendary
frontier scout Jim Nugent, whose fame as an Indian scout
was only exceeded by his unsavory reputation.

Upon meeting him, Isabella forgot about the gossip, "for his manner was that of a chivalrous gentleman, his accent refined, and his language easy and elegant." In a letter to her sister, Hennie, she described him as a man about forty-five, broad and thickset, with deep-set blue-gray eyes, well-marked eyebrows, a handsome aquiline nose, and tawny curly hair. His face "might have been modeled in marble" except for the loss of one eye due to an unfortunate encounter with a grizzly bear.

An Irishman born in Canada, Jim proved to be well read, gregarious, and always courteous to women, but given to "dark moods" when drinking. With a bloody past and a dismal future, he worked as a trapper, living in a hut that "looked like the den of a wild beast." Isabella was attracted nonetheless, and Jim promised to lead her and two companions on the Longs Peak trip. In the meanwhile, she found quarters in a cozy little cabin reserved for summer guests.

The spectacular Longs Peak climb proved far more difficult than Isabella anticipated. "Had I known that the ascent was a real mountaineering feat, I should not have felt the slightest ambition to perform it," she later wrote. Realizing that her inexperience slowed the party's progress, Isabella offered to forgo the final trek to the summit, but Jim refused to leave her behind. "Like a bale of goods," he pulled her up the mountain.

The view must have been breathtaking from 14,000 feet, a magnificent panorama of snowy peaks and basins, gray-green rolling plains, and the sleepy, winding Big

Thompson River. Romantically, they carved their initials on a food tin and tucked it into a fissure. During the descent, Isabella suffered bruised ankles from falls and her clothing caught on the rocks. At one point she found herself "hanging by my frock," which Jim severed with a hunting knife, sending her tumbling into a ravine filled with feathery soft snow.

"Sometimes I drew myself on my hands and knees, sometimes crawled, sometimes Jim pulled me up by my arms or a lariat, and sometimes I stood on his shoulders or he made steps for me with his feet and hands," she wrote. "But at six we stood on the 'Notch' in the splendor of the sinking sun, all color deepening, all peaks glorifying, all shadows purpling, all peril past."

Back at camp, Isabella and Jim developed a rapport that led him to reveal the painful story of his past. The son of a British officer stationed in Montreal, he had been an ungovernable teenager who fell in love at seventeen to a girl his mother found unsuitable. The young woman's subsequent death led him to alcohol and a lawless life, particulars of which he related vividly to Isabella. She found the gruesome details titillating and horrifying, seeing him through a Byronic haze as "brilliant, and full of the light and fitfulness of genius," a man "with blood on his hands and murder in his heart." Although she sometimes suspected him of putting on a show for her benefit, the dramatic performance must have been convincing. If the pair became physically intimate, the secret died with them. Isabella's letters to her sister were scrupulously edited before publication, and some topics were still off limits for Victorian women, no matter how independent.

The relationship faltered when Isabella returned to Estes Park after a brief Colorado Springs jaunt to find Jim in a "black fit." According to her account, he confessed his love for her in agony. "You've stirred the better nature in me too late! I cannot reform." Isabella was deeply moved, but realistic. "He is so lovable and fascinating yet so terrible ... He is a man whom any woman might love, but no sane woman would marry." Finally she sent him a note written in shaky hand: "There can be nothing between us but constraint."

In early December, Jim escorted Isabella to the stage-coach bound for Greeley. They spent their last evening together at a settlement called Saint Louis, where the landlady felt honored to have the notorious "Mountain Jim" as a guest, "as if he had been the President." In the evening, Jim recited poetry to Isabella and promised to give up whiskey and the "reputation of a desperado,"—ostensibly for her sake.

She rode Jim's Arab mare as far as a Greeley stage station, where they encountered a tourist named Fodder, whom she had met earlier. She compared him contemptuously to her mountain man: "He [Fodder] had expressed a great wish to go to Estes Park and to hunt with Mountain Jim, if it would be safe. He was now dressed in the extreme of English dandyism, and when I introduced them, he put out a small hand cased in perfectly fitting lemon-colored kid gloves. As the trapper stood there in his grotesque rags and odds and ends of apparel, his gentlemanliness of deportment brought into relief the innate vulgarity of a rich parvenu."

Watching Jim slowly lead her mare back to Estes, "his golden hair yellow in the sunshine," Isabella never thought to end their relationship. But just six months later, she learned that Jim had been shot and killed during a quarrel with a neighbor. In Switzerland by then, Isabella claimed that he appeared to her in spirit form, presumably to say good-bye. Later she rationalized their brief affair: "Don't let anybody think that I was in love with Mountain Jim … but it was pity and yearning to save him that I felt." Isabella later published her heavily edited letters to Hennie in *A Lady's Life in the Rocky Mountains*, a beautifully written account of her Colorado expedition.

While visiting her sister in Edinburgh in 1878, Isabella found herself being courted by the family physician, Dr. John Bishop. Faced with the prospect of marriage and curtailment of her freedom, Isabella discovered that her old spinal problems mysteriously resurfaced. Possibly the attraction of Dr. Bishop's "reverential tenderness" paled in comparison to the raw passion of a man like Jim Nugent, and a bad back seemed as good an excuse as any. At any rate, after apologetically expressing concern that she might become "an invalid wife," the lady immediately fled to Japan and Malaysia.

When Hennie suddenly died of typhoid in 1881, grief and loneliness apparently got the best of Isabella, and she agreed to marry Bishop. But at fifty, Isabella had no intention of trading in her hiking boots. After her husband's death just four years later, she took off again for "the country which lies beneath China and North India," intending to climb the plateau of Lesser Tibet and build a hospital in Bishop's memory. The wandering continued for years, taking her from India and Persia to China and beyond. Isabella established hospitals in remote regions, and in 1892 she became the first woman ever elected a fellow of the Royal Geographic Society. According to a friend, Agnes Grainger Stewart, Lady Isabella's intellect, humor, and zest for living remained undiminished until she died of heart disease in 1904. She undoubtedly retained fond memories of that glorious Colorado autumn and her romantic interlude with the notorious Mountain Jim Nugent.

CHAPTER II

# Adventurers, Gamblers, and Shady Ladies

### ✒

## The Royal Sting

*Countess Katrina and Count Henri Murat*

On May 7, 1859, the Leavenworth and Pikes Peak Stage thundered into Denver City, connecting the isolated mining camp for the first time to the outside world. To celebrate the occasion, townsfolk proudly hung the city's first flag from a fifty-foot pine pole near the new stage stop. The all-American creation had been handsewn by Countess Katrina Murat, one of the settlement's more colorful and bizarre characters. From Parisian garments borrowed from her trousseau, Katrina had fashioned the red stripes from a merino skirt and the white stripes and stars from a silk petticoat. A blue flannel dress provided a background for the stars.

Katrina and her husband, Count Henri Murat, had been among the first Denver pioneers in 1858. Countess Murat, the daughter a prosperous Prussian vintner, was born Katrina Wolf in Baden-Baden on the Rhine in 1824. Count Henri Murat claimed to be the nephew of Joachim Murat, the French marshal who became Bonaparte's king of Naples. According to his account, Henri left France *tout de suite* when the Bourbon kings put a price on his head. Hidden in a load of hay, he traveled to Germany, where he found work on Katrina's father's estate. The couple fell in love, even though Henri was technically a political refugee. After hearing of the count's distinguished background, Katrina's parents blessed their marriage and the couple set sail for the United States in 1848. The ten years between their departure from Prussia and their arrival in Denver remain something of a mystery.

Another popular tale suggests that Katrina had been married and widowed before she met Henri. According to this version, the couple met in 1854, when the count was working as a San Francisco dentist. Katrina had crossed the plains a few years earlier with her first husband, a man named Stolsenberger, who left her a $75,000 inheritance. After a brief courtship, Henri and Katrina married and disposed of her fortune during a glorious European honeymoon.

In any case, the Murats joined the Pikes Peak gold rush and headed west to Colorado with visions of gold nuggets dancing in their heads. They settled first in Montana City, which was located seven miles from Denver up the Platte River. On November 5, 1858, Henri wrote the following to a business associate named Zillard:

On Thursday morning we arrived here all in good health. We had the most beautiful and pleasant weather the whole trip, with the exception of two thunderstorms … My wife is well and getting fat. She looks as blooming and fresh as a maiden, so well has the free air of the prairies agreed with her … My dear friend, we are not sorry for coming out here, for in the first place, it is the most lovely country you ever saw. To our right there is a range of mountains where the Platte River emerges. It must be the most beautiful sight. Gold is found everywhere you stick your shovel and paying from five to ten cents to the pan … My frau is the first white woman out here and will make money by washing clothes, which will pay her perhaps fifty cents apiece …

In Denver, Henri and Katrina set up Denver's first Christmas tree, brought in fresh from the mountains. The sweet-smelling spruce was decorated with small candles, which sat in holders made from wooden blocks and pieces of wire. Tiny gingerbread figures also adorned the tree. On Christmas Eve, the Murats invited the town's two other families over to their small cabin for refreshments and Christmas carols. On the following day, several miners joined the royal family for Christmas dinner, which consisted of dried, sliced potatoes, dried green beans, black-eyed peas, and venison. Countess Katrina, a wonderful cook, made compote of several kinds of dried fruits and served gingerbread cookies with the dessert.

By 1859, the Murats had moved to the Auraria side of
Cherry Creek, where they became proprietors of the Eldorado
Hotel with a partner named David Smoke. Denver's first
hostelry was quite primitive, built of raw timber with a dirt

One of the first white women in Denver, Countess Katrina Murat
fashioned the settlement's first American flag from garments in her
trousseau. *(Courtesy of the Colorado Historical Society, #F-7925)*

floor and furnished with a simple fireplace, homemade stick furniture, and buffalo robes that served as beds. A tower atop the hotel roof gave Henri the first crack at spotting approaching wagon trains; supposedly, he would ride out to greet guests in tails and a top hat. Within three months the partners sold the hotel, which then became the Union Bakery.

Although the life of a frontier innkeeper must have been quite a setback after the castles of Europe, Katrina quickly became accustomed to pioneer life. Besides, she was a great cook. Before long, the Murats moved to the Denver side of the creek, where they operated a bakery. Later, Henri opened a barbershop on Larimer Street, where he charged Horace Greeley $5 for a haircut. Katrina also took the famous visitor to the cleaners, billing the penurious editor $3 to launder a few shirts. She later made up for it by providing quarters in her cabin when he had difficulty sleeping at the Eldorado "due to the promiscuous firing of pistols." Greeley described Henri as "the tall Italian in solemn black, smoking a large meerschaum pipe" and wryly characterized him as "one man in camp determined to make the most of his opportunities."

The following year the Murats took off for California. They generally traveled by horseback; fortunately, Katrina had become an accomplished rider. She also learned to shoot a rifle with frightening accuracy, a helpful skill during skirmishes with the Indians. Fortune never smiled on the Murats for long, however—they were in and out of money all their lives. On one occasion, after they'd struck it rich at some enterprise, they headed back to Denver with more than $50,000. This time they traveled by stagecoach, but Katrina had become so heavy that it took two men to hoist her into the coach. The weight gain wasn't totally due to her cooking, however. To fool would-be thieves, the countess hid gold dust and coins in buckskin bags sewn to the inside of her skirts. The ruse was successful, but the belts chafed her thighs and left her scarred for life.

With the spoils of one windfall, the Murats purchased Criterion Hall, a saloon formerly owned by gambler Charley Harrison. Although the Criterion had an unsavory reputation, they hoped to turn the establishment into a respectable business. By 1863, they had given up and moved on to Virginia City, where they opened the Continental Restaurant. A definite improvement over the Eldorado, the Continental served champagne and homemade ice cream and featured Katrina's tasty pies and pastries.

The Murats moved to and from Denver, spending their flush times in Europe and California. They were particularly fond of casinos and in later years moved to Palmer Lake, where Henri hoped to create an American Monte Carlo. After 1876 their fortunes declined, and Henri began drinking heavily. Katrina divorced him in 1881, and he died flat broke a few years later. Katrina built a cabin near Palmer Lake where she took in boarders and embraced the simple life. Well respected by the community, she lingered until 1910, supported by the Pioneer Ladies Aid Society.

Their original Auraria establishment, the Eldorado, fell into disuse over the years. In 1939, wrecking crews demolishing a house at 1249 Tenth Street discovered a shell of hewn logs, which several experts believed to be the original Eldorado. *Denver Post* heiress May Bonfils purchased the building and moved it to her estate in Lakewood, which has since been demolished and replaced by a museum. After Bonfils's death, Historic Denver and the Colorado State Historical Society moved the house to the basement of the Colorado History Museum, where it has remained. Further investigation proved that the structure was not really the Eldorado, but the building next door.

## A Date with Destiny
*Ada LaMont and Charley Harrison*

*I*n the summer of 1858, a beautiful, dark-eyed young woman joined her husband on a wagon train heading for the Pikes Peak region. Born into a respectable family in the Midwest, she had been married for two years to a young minister from her church. To all appearances, they were quite happily married and devoted to one another. As the wagons crept over the sunbaked prairie, they made plans to build a church once they had settled in the new territory.

One night the clergyman mysteriously disappeared, along with a young woman reputed to be a prostitute. Since no trace of either could be found, people on the wagon train assumed that the two had run off together.

The minister's young wife continued on to the goldfields, silent and brooding. When the party reached the outskirts of Denver, she turned her wagon toward Indian Row in Auraria. She announced to her shocked fellow passengers that she intended to abandon her former life and open the town's first brothel under the name Ada LaMont. She declared that anyone looking for a little fun would always find her available. Still in her teens, Ada did a brisk business in a settlement composed primarily of men. Within a year she left Indian

Row and moved into a two-story house on Arapahoe Street. Apparently some of her early religious upbringing must have made an impression, since she operated an honest business. According to reports, her employees never stole from clients and she served the best liquor in town.

Ada met Charley Harrison early in 1859, and the pair immediately became an item. Taken with her spirit and good looks, Charley escorted her to parties and celebrations and frequently stepped in when aggressive or abusive clients threatened her establishment. Harrison was probably in his early forties at the time, handsome and stocky with a well-trimmed black beard. According to legend, he always carried a pair of pearl-handled Colt revolvers, which he used when he found it necessary. During his brief two years in Denver, he apparently found it necessary only twice—not bad compared to the multitude of shootings credited to his name.

A southerner by birth, Harrison began his gambling career dealing faro in New York during the 1840s. He showed up in California around 1854, but fled the Golden Gate when San Francisco vigilantes unceremoniously hung two of his gaming brethren. Harrison drifted from Montana and Idaho to Utah, where he rescued a fellow gambler named Tom Hunt from a Mormon lynching party. Still on the run, he showed up in Denver in January 1859.

Brawling and lawless, Denver City welcomed gamblers of all kinds, and Charley immediately took his place as their leader. After dealing monte in the Denver House for a few months, he bought one of the town's more accommodating establishments, the Criterion, on 15th and Larimer. The wickedest among Denver's thirty-one shady saloons, the Criterion offered dancing, drinking, gambling, sleeping rooms, and other amusements requested by lusty frontiersmen.

Decent folk avoided Ada and Charley, although Harrison's stock went up after he made peace with *Rocky Mountain News* publisher William Newton Byers. Their dispute began when Charley shot down an African American named Stark, who had apparently insulted the Dixie-born gambler by calling him by his first name. After Ada bribed the jury with $5,000 to release Harrison, Byers wrote an enraged editorial in the *Rocky Mountain News* denouncing the killing as "wanton and unprovoked" and Charley "unfit to live in ... a civilized community."

Many of Charley's supporters favored eliminating the pesky editor once and for all, including a motley gang called the Bummers. Taking the high road instead, Charley and his enthusiastic comrades arranged a meeting with Byers. Several witnesses, including probate court judge Seymour Waggonner, swore to Byers that Stark had attacked first with a bowie knife. The *News* subsequently printed a revised version of the incident, adding irritably, "the public seems so well satisfied of the justification of Mr. Harrison that we presume nothing will be done."

A subsequent investigation by the newly formed Denver City Vigilance Committee (infiltrated by another group of Charley's friends called the Stranglers) exonerated Harrison of all blame. The Bummers, however, remained unsatisfied. A

few days later, the disgruntled rabble invaded the *Rocky
Mountain News* office and marched the nervous editor back
to the Criterion. Charley slipped Byers out the back door,
advising the editor to get ready for more trouble. When the
frustrated Bummers launched a second attack on Byers, marshal Tom Pollock, the vigilantes, and the Stranglers tossed
them out of town. The incident, particularly Charley's repu-
diation of the Bummers, actually enhanced the gambler's
reputation, and soon he was catering to Denver's better element, such as it was.

Harrison's career took a downward spiral after the
Criterion hosted a group of representatives who met in
Denver to establish the Jefferson Territorial Provisional
Legislature. Business had been brisk until a group from
Golden took control of the legislature and maneuvered its
adjournment to the rival town. When Charley exchanged
hostile words with a man named Riley, he foolishly chal-
lenged Denver's gambling prince to a duel. Although Riley
apologized and called off the fight, a rancher named Hill had
made a special trip to Denver just to see the showdown.
Irritated that the spectacle had been canceled, Hill got on
Charley's bad side by insulting Harrison's bartender. Guns
were drawn and soon James Hill was on boot hill, joining
Charley's first casualty, the unfortunate Mr. Stark.
Understandably, the gambler's reputation for sensitivity was
making everybody a little nervous. Even editor Byers, who
owed Charley Harrison his life, thought things had gone too
far. He did allow the gambler to tell his side of the story in

the *News*, and once again Harrison got away with murder, or so many folks thought.

Meanwhile, things were not going well for Charley and Ada, who was now sharing her paramour with an alcoholic newcomer, a pretty young blonde named Lizz Greer. They quarreled frequently and at one point ended the relationship, at least temporarily. When the Civil War broke out in April 1861, Charley enraged fellow citizens who supported the Union (which constituted a majority) by making the Criterion the headquarters of southern sympathizers. Soon an altercation with Company B of the First Colorado Volunteers led to the arrest of Harrison and friends on a charge of rebellion. Since Charley still had a few friends left in Denver, the judge found him guilty of a lesser charge of obstructing justice and fined him $5,000. Ordered to "git out of town," he sold the Criterion and left Denver for good in September 1861.

Harrison headed back to his homeland and immediately enlisted in the Confederate Army. A natural leader, he became a captain and rose within two years to the rank of colonel. He assumed command of the Fourth Missouri Cavalry, showing as much mercy to the Union Army as he had to Mr. Stark and Mr. Hill.

Still irritated by his treatment in Denver, Harrison convinced his superiors that the town contained a veritable gold mine of supplies and ammunition, which the Confederacy desperately needed. He formed a raiding party and set out across the prairie with high hopes and nineteen men.

Unfortunately, Charley hadn't counted on the Osage Indians. The tribe held a grudge against Confederate guerrillas who had driven them from Texas and Arkansas, and thus had sworn their loyalty to the Union. On Lightning Creek in southeastern Kansas, they attacked Harrison's troops, killing and scalping eighteen Confederates, including Charley.

Ada's life also ended soon, dramatically if not heroically. Depressed by Charley's departure and subsequent demise, she soon suffered another shock. A group of travelers had discovered her husband's remains on the prairie, along with those of the missing woman. The minister's skeleton had a hole in the back of the head and a bullet lodged in the skull. In a bundle of rags, someone found the gift that she had once given her beloved—a Bible with her inscription still legible. Deeply affected and filled with remorse, Ada began to drink heavily. Business went downhill, and she boarded up her establishment and moved on. Eventually she drifted into Georgetown, where she died of starvation in the midst of the silver boom.

# The Confederate Mata Hari

*Belle Siddons and Archie McLaughlin*

*A* social butterfly with a taste for intrigue, Belle Siddons came from a prominent family in Saint Louis. A southern loyalist, she agreed to spy for the Confederacy during the Civil War, although her family ostensibly supported the Union. When Belle was arrested in 1862, the not-so-naive ingénue boasted that she had supplied Gen. Nathan B. Forest with information vital to the war effort. After keeping the lady in custody for several months, the Union Army tossed her out of Missouri until the war ended.

Belle later married a surgeon named Hallett, who died of yellow fever in 1869. The doctor had a fondness for gambling, which inspired his young widow to begin a new career in Wichita, Kansas, as a professional gambler. Calling herself Madam Vestal, she became one of the most accomplished blackjack dealers in the West, at one time operating a tented gambling house in Denver. Leaving Colorado in 1876, she followed the gold rush to the Black Hills, where she took the name Lurlene Monte Verde. One Deadwood City reporter romantically described her as "a flawlessly groomed beauty, artfully jeweled and gowned."

Two years later, Belle had the misfortune to fall in love with a stagecoach robber named Archie McLaughlin. Brushing up her espionage skills, she supplied him with inside information about gold shipments. The sheriff must have caught on, because several of Archie's gang members were subsequently wounded in an unsuccessful robbery. Like a trooper, Belle went to the hideout to help one of the thieves, who had been seriously wounded. Her ungrateful patient later testified against his cohorts, including Archie.

The McLaughlin gang broke out of jail and tried to escape to Cheyenne, but they were captured and sent back to Deadwood via stagecoach. Vigilantes stopped the stage outside of Deadwood, kidnapped the prisoners, and in the fashion of a Clint Eastwood Western, "hung 'em high." The inconsolable Belle fell into a deep depression from which she never recovered. She closed her gambling operation and moved aimlessly through western boomtowns, appearing at various times in Leadville and other mining camps. Addicted to alcohol and opium, she died in San Francisco at age forty.

🦋

# The Grande Dame
# of Market Street
*Mattie Silks and Cort Thompson*

*A*lthough crimson sunsets and purple sage provide a romantic setting for Western movies, not many prospectors descending upon Colorado boom towns qualified as Zane Grey material. Between gold grubbing, fighting, and drinking, most were too busy to think about love, although sex often ran a close second to liquor. Give or take a few genuine pioneers traveling with their families, the first women in any boomtown were generally prostitutes. Ladies in search of more stable relationships usually waited until the dust settled, then had their predecessors restricted to a few blocks on the livelier side of town.

As mining camps grew into towns and cities, the parlor house became a preferred business setting for the youngest and prettiest "soiled doves." Clients who could afford the price enjoyed certain amenities in a higher-class brothel, including decent food and liquor, attractive surroundings, and frequently a disease-free partner. Madams who operated these upscale establishments were usually astute businesswomen like Mattie Silks, Queen of Denver's red-light district.

A farm girl with lofty ambitions, Mattie hailed from Terre Haute or Gary, Indiana. She began her career just after the Civil War, operating her first bordello at nineteen. She headed west with the Kansas Pacific Railroad during the 1870s and set up her first Colorado "tent bordello" northwest of Boulder. After moving her entourage to Georgetown, she married a man named Silks, either Casey (a railroad man) or George (a gambler), who either died or left town. A petite, curvy blonde with curly hair and an engaging smile, Mattie often boasted that she had never worked as a prostitute, preferring to leave the more mundane tasks to her girls. With a diamond cross as her trademark and a twinkle in her eye, she dominated the local market.

Although bright and capable in most respects, Mattie had truly bad taste in men. When the relationship ended with Silks, her next big mistake was Cortez D. Thompson, a gambler/athlete with a fondness for drink and a powerful aversion to work. Dapper, good-looking, and well built, Thomson (aka "Cort") told folks he had ridden with Quantrill's Raiders during the Civil War, an assertion difficult to disprove. He finally found his niche as a foot racer, a popular sport that appealed to the Colorado gaming set. Although Cort occasionally threw a race when offered the right bribe, he cut a handsome figure in tights. He took off with Mattie's heart when she saw him race for Georgetown's Silver Queen volunteer fire department. Leaving a wife and daughter behind, he set up housekeeping with Mattie. In 1876, the couple moved to Denver, where Mattie became the proprietress of several cribs and sporting houses on Market Street.

Although Cort had a wandering eye, beat her occasionally, and gambled away both their earnings, Mattie adored him. She supported him without complaint, although she did once tell a friend that if Cort insisted on playing cards, she wished he'd get better at it. A legendary tale about the red-light lovers took place in August 1877, when Mattie supposedly fought a duel for Cort's attentions with another madam, Kate Fulton.

The ruckus began after Cort defeated an accomplished rival in the 125-yard dash, netting Mattie several thousand dollars. To celebrate, the couple threw a party at old Denver Park, where Cherry Creek flows into the South Platte. With plenty of liquor everyone had a jolly good time until late into the night, when Mattie noticed Cort paying a little too much attention to Kate.

As a heated argument evolved into a wrestling match, someone suggested that the ladies fight a duel. In the true spirit the Old West, both women were handed pistols and ordered to pace off. (More imaginative male historians later suggested that Mattie and Kate fought bare-breasted.) When the proverbial smoke cleared, the ladies had suffered only a few minor bruises. The only person shot (presumably by accident) turned out to be the troublemaker Thomson, felled by a bullet in the neck. Mattie nursed him back to health and took him on a long vacation.

Denver newspapers never mentioned the duel, characterizing the event as a quarrel between two scarlet sisters that escalated into a free-for-all. According to the journalists' version, Cort's injury actually occurred as he rode out of the park in his carriage. Supposedly, an unknown assailant fired the shot with Cort's own pistol, which he had drawn and dropped during the scuffle. The culprit may have been Kate's lover, Sam Thatcher, who was understandably annoyed at Cort for breaking her nose. Madam Fulton took the next train to Kansas City after the altercation, but returned the following month. Obviously a slow learner, she quarreled with Mattie again. Weary of it all, Mattie broke Kate's nose once more, then had her arrested for assault.

Mattie and Cort were finally married in July 1884, after the death of his wife in Georgetown. Thompson continued to gamble, foot race, and get into fights, while Mattie paid the bills. Hoping to entice her husband away from the gaming tables, Mattie bought a large spread near Wray, where she stabled racehorses. Known only as Mrs. C. D. Thomson by her country neighbors, she visited the ranch often. Even in the boondocks, however, Cort couldn't stay out of trouble. He tried his hand at cattle rustling, and then sprinted off to Texas before he could be arrested. The Julesberg sheriff caught up with him in the Lone Star State and tossed him in jail. Disgusted, Mattie had an affair with a railroad tycoon from New York.

Mattie and Cort's relationship reached a crisis when she caught him living with her former friend from Leadville, another madam named Lillie Dab. Mattie filed for divorce, justly accusing Cort of wife beating, drinking, and philandering. Perhaps she was less concerned about his longtime abuse than his attempts to sell the ranch, which she had unwisely put in his name. After Cort agreed to relinquish the property, she dismissed her suit and the couple reconciled. They took a jaunt to Europe, and then in 1897 tried their luck in the Klondike. Neither could abide the weather, and they returned to Denver after three months, $38,000 richer thanks to Mattie's business interests.

By 1900, they were living separately, Cort in Wray and Mattie in Denver. On his fifty-third birthday, Cort went on a final bender and died of drug and alcohol abuse a month later. Although Mattie sobbed that she could never live without him, she buried him at Fairmount Cemetery and went on with her life. Always a sucker for a good-looking man, she soon took up with her foreman in Wray, a redheaded giant named John Dillon Ready. "Handsome Jack" soon relocated to Denver to become her protector, bouncer, and general man-about-the-bordello. Several years younger than Mattie, he was a fancy dresser and an athlete like Cort.

In 1911, Mattie purchased a property she had long coveted, Jennie Rogers's House of Mirrors. Unfortunately, the timing was wrong. Denver closed the sporting houses shortly after Colorado enacted Prohibition in 1916 (four years ahead of the rest of the country) and Mattie sold the House of Mirrors to Japanese businessmen. She converted her property at 1916 Market Street into the Silks Hotel, which never quite worked out. John found employment as a telegraph operator and livestock dealer, marrying Mattie in 1924 when she was in her late seventies.

Denver's most popular ex-madam broke her hip in 1926 and remained confined to a wheelchair for the next two years. High-spirited to the end, she tried to stand up during a Christmas party, fell, and broke her hip again. She died at Denver General Hospital on January 7, 1929. After earning and losing millions during her lifetime, she left only $4,000 in real estate and $2,500 in jewelry. Her estate was divided equally between Ready and her adopted daughter, Theresa, probably Cort's child by his first wife. Mattie was buried under her real name, Martha A. Ready, at Fairmount Cemetery, next to the unmarked grave of her beloved Cort. For reasons unknown, "Handsome Jack" lies about a block north.

&

# A Red-Light
# Romeo and Juliet
*Lois Lovell and Unknown Lover*

Lois Lovell was said to be the younger sister of Lillas Lovell, an elegant madam who worked the mining towns of Leadville and Creede. A highly intelligent businesswoman known as "Creede Lil," she came to Denver in 1906 and successfully operated an elegant parlor house at 2020 Market Street. Reportedly a professional singer at one time, Lil had a beautiful voice. She became one of the richest women on Market Street, blithely parading down Market Street in elaborate costumes and thousands of dollars worth of jewelry.

Within a few months, Lil invited her younger sister, Lois, to join her in Denver. Before long, Lois fell in love with one of the patrons, a handsome young gentleman from a respected Denver family. Although her lover proposed marriage, Lois demurred, fearing (à la Camille in *La Traviata*) that the union would disgrace his family. Refusing to be discouraged, he left town on a business trip, promising to return. After he had been gone for several weeks, Lois became despondent and committed suicide.

Lois's sweetheart returned to Denver, determined to marry his reluctant ladylove and take her back to California so they could start a new life. When told of her death, he quietly asked to be taken to the cemetery where she had been buried. Looking down at her grave, he pulled out a pistol, put the muzzle to his head, and fired.

ॐ

# A Cripple Creek Jewel
*Pearl DeVere and the Mystery Millionaire*

*I*n the early 1890s, few experts believed that the Teller
County gold strike would amount to much. By 1894,
however, Cripple Creek had become one of the few bright
spots in Colorado's economic wasteland, producing $5 mil-
lion a year and churning out millionaires by the score.
Eventually, the mining district became one of the largest gold
regions the world has ever seen, taking second place in production only to South Africa.

Madam Pearl DeVere blazed into Cripple Creek in
1893, shortly after the strike had turned the two tiny settle-
ments of Hayden Placer and Fremont into a single, rowdy
mining camp. Some said that she came from Denver, where
the Silver Panic had severely reduced her clientele. A lady
with style, Pearl quickly became a local celebrity. Strikingly
beautiful with long, dark eyelashes and auburn hair, she
would race through the streets in a single-seated carriage with
bright red wheels, elegantly attired in a different outfit every
day. Before long, the glamorous lady caught the eye of
wealthy miner and mill owner C. B. Flynn, who married her
despite her profession (or perhaps because of it). When the
great Cripple Creek fire of 1896 ruined Flynn financially, he

took off for Mexico. Since business was booming, Pearl stayed put.

Soon Madam DeVere earned enough cash to build a two-story brick parlor house on Myers Avenue, the town's infamous five-block red-light district. With a touch of cynicism, Pearl named the establishment "the Old Homestead." Desiring the most elegant bawdy house on the street, she decorated the downstairs lavishly with red velvet chairs and crystal chandeliers. To grace the banquet room, hand-painted wallpaper with traces of laurel had been shipped from France at $134 a roll. The Old Homestead even flaunted two bathrooms in a town where most folks still used an outhouse. According to a 1900 census, the staff consisted of a cook, a housekeeper, two chambermaids, two butlers, a musician, and five female "boarders." The parlor house required a letter of introduction for a visit that cost from $50 to $100.

At a time when career options were limited for women in mining towns, between 250 and 300 prostitutes plied their trade on Myers Avenue. Rather than discourage the thriving business, Cripple Creek officials collected a tax of $16 a month for each madam and $6 for each girl. Regular physical exams were required, which kept consciences relatively clear and the town's coffers full. Perhaps the Old Homestead could be considered "the best of the worst" for the young women themselves, although prostitutes often became addicted to drugs and alcohol and were frequently victims of abuse.

Pearl had a legion of admirers and always entertained in style. One June evening in 1897 she threw a special party, supposedly for a new lover. For the gala affair she had turned the parlor room into a botanical paradise with orchids, gardenias, and mimosa shipped in from Mexico. The Homestead brought in two orchestras from Denver to provide accompaniment for the latest dances. According to an article in the *Cripple Creek Gold Rush*, Pearl wore "an eight hundred dollar ball gown of shell pink chiffon, encrusted with sequins and seed pearls, sent direct to her from Paris." The gentleman in question may have been Winfield Scott Stratton, owner of the Independence Mine and the richest of the Cripple Creek tycoons. A former carpenter turned prospector, he reputedly hated women after suffering an unfortunate marriage. The handsome, silver-haired bachelor generally restricted his female friends to high-class prostitutes.

Pearl and her friend supposedly had a terrible quarrel that night. One story eliminates Stratton as the suitor, maintaining that the lovers fought because Pearl wanted the man to divorce his wife. Afterward, the Homestead's mistress seemed in high spirits during the party, laughing merrily and drinking several glasses of French champagne. While her guests were still celebrating, Pearl complained that she felt ill and that her nerves were "all unstrung." Refusing offers of assistance she went upstairs and took an extra dose of morphine to help her sleep. Accidentally or otherwise, she never woke up again. According to the newspaper, an unnamed wealthy patron discovered her body, then immediately left for Denver "on business."

The sheriff took possession of the Old Homestead, and preparations began for Pearl's funeral. When her sister arrived from Evanston, Illinois, the lady took one look at the dyed red hair on the corpse and left town. Apparently Pearl had written to the family that she was a designer who dressed the wives of the gold kings. Although the town of Cripple Creek was prepared to bury Pearl in style, an anonymous $1,000 donation came from Denver at the last minute to cover expenses. The sister may have regretted her hasty decision and provided the funds, or the money might have come from C. B. Flynn. The mysterious lover who fled back to Denver the night she died might also have contributed. In any event, Pearl's funeral turned into a grand affair. She journeyed to Mount Pisgah Cemetery in a lavender casket covered with red and white roses. A twenty-piece Elks Club band accompanied the entourage, including most of the lodge members, four mounted policeman, and several carriages full of "coworkers." As the casket was lowered into the ground, a lonely coronet played "Good-bye, Little Girl, Good-bye." Pearl had been thirty-six, a dangerous age for sex goddesses in the days before botox.

The Old Homestead has since been converted into a museum, perhaps the only one ever dedicated to the proprietress of a brothel. Artifacts include a ruby glass "*Gone with the Wind*" lamp, a corset chair, and a poker table that may have belonged to Cripple Creek gambler Johnny Nolan. Pearl's grave can still be found in the southeastern quadrant of the Mount Pisgah Cemetery. During the 1950s, a heart-shaped stone replaced the wooden grave marker, which is now in the Cripple Creek District Museum.

❧

# A HOT TIME
# IN THE OLD TOWN TONIGHT

Old-fashioned dance halls were often called "hurdy-gurdy" houses, named after a German musical instrument similar to a hand organ. Bawdy houses and gambling parlors had their own agendas, but dance halls existed only to sell overpriced liquor. The young women employed by such establishments often were recent escapees from farms and mills back East, trying to better their lives while maintaining a smidgen of respectability.

The musical social gatherings were usually held in a shabby building or large tent with a dirt floor and benches on both sides. An old upright piano, a fiddle or two, or maybe even a brass instrument would provide musical accompaniment. The bar offered a limited selection of cheap liquor such as Taos Lightning, a potent wheat whiskey enhanced by tobacco, gunpowder, chili peppers, and occasionally a few grasshoppers. As antifreeze it was reportedly quite effective, converting the shyest cowpoke into a veritable John Travolta.

Girls usually wore heavy boots to protect their toes, a precaution that became more significant as the evening wore on and the customers drank on. Depending on the sophistication of the establishment, the hurdy-gurdy gal might wear anything from an evening gown to a muslin dress, but shorter skirts were usually required. After the dance, the lady would lead her partner to the bar, where he would purchase their drinks at an exorbitant price. The girl got a commission on the drinks and kept half her earnings from the dance floor. Since a drunken hurdy could be pretty deadly during a polka, the lady usually got watered-down tea.

Many dance halls had strict rules and discouraged further fraternization with the customers. A few hurdy-girls managed to marry and start a new life, but often they shared the fate of their less respectable sisters in the parlor houses. Some became drug addicts or alcoholics, while others died violently or committed suicide.

Hurdy girls and their customers take a break at Crapper Jack's saloon in Cripple Creek. *(Courtesy of the Denver Public Library, Western History Collection, #X-652)*

In Cripple Creek, most of the dance halls were located in the red-light district on Myers Avenue. By the late 1890s, the town had seventy-three saloons, many with ten-piece bands and lots of dancing girls. Before each show began, they would all parade downtown as advertisement, often accompanied by the popular tune, "There'll Be a Hot Time in the Old Town Tonight." According to a popular story, on April 25, 1896, that song became particularly meaningful when a bartender got into a heated argument with his girlfriend on the second floor of the Central Dance Hall. He slapped her, she fought back, and during the fracas they knocked over a lighted gasoline stove. The wooden floor caught fire and flames spread so rapidly that some of the girls upstairs had to escape by sliding down a rope. The ensuing blaze left 1,500 people homeless and effectively eliminated most of the town's business district. Reportedly, the lovebirds kissed and made up afterward.

## ✌

# Three Queens for a King

*Frances Barbour, Margaret Jane, Helen Brown,
and Ed Chase*

*I*f Ed Chase had never existed, a Hollywood scriptwriter
would have invented him. Overlord of Denver gambling
for nearly fifty years, Chase had movie-idol good looks, prematurely silver hair, and riveting blue eyes that could make a
woman's heart flutter or an adversary's blood run cold.
Although he loved women, his amorous exploits generally
ended in disaster—until he found the one woman who could
keep him interested for life.

Ed Chase was an enigma to the gaming community,
with a background that seemed too sophisticated for a back-
water boomtown like early Denver. Born in December
1836, Ed grew up near Saratoga Springs, New York, where
his affluent family ran an upscale hotel and raised thorough-
bred horses. His mother, Maria Chase, was a Quaker. Ed's
parents sent him to Zenovia Seminary, but at nineteen he
lost interest in school. Bolstered by a $1,500 stake he'd won
in an all-night poker game, he headed West with a friend
named Samuel N. Wood. They found Colorado's weather
too chilly and traveled on to Montana, where warm winds
supposedly made for a milder climate. After experiencing

freezing temperatures more typical of winter in the Big Sky Country, they quickly returned to Colorado.

At the Clear Creek diggings, Ed and Sam tried prospecting. While Sam went on to become a leader in the mining industry, Ed gave up and took a job at the Ford Brothers store in Golden. Joined by his brother John he successfully promoted prizefights as a sideline. The Chase brothers came to Denver around 1861, just about the time gambling kingpin

Handsome gambler Ed Chase had problems with
women until he met vaudeville performer
Frances Minerva Barbour.
*(Courtesy of the Colorado Historical Society, #22-575)*

Charley Harrison was heading back East to join the Confederacy. Ed Chase filled the vacancy nicely.

The personable young gambler knew how to make friends. His original enterprise, a tent saloon on Blake Street, had been blessed at its opening by the presence of Col. John M. Chivington, an elder in the Methodist church. Chivington later gained notoriety for the appalling Sand Creek Massacre, the slaughter of more than two hundred peaceful Cheyenne and Arapaho, mostly women and children. Although Chase participated in the raid, he preferred not to discuss it in later years. On the positive side, Ed's many good deeds included rescuing two young men named Moses Hallett and Vincent D. Markham by stalling an angry mob until they had time to escape. Both boys later embraced the judicial system, with Markham serving on the bench and Hallett becoming a federal judge.

Chase's gambling enterprise prospered and soon he and his partner, Hub Healey, moved across Blake Street at the request of several prominent businessmen who wanted a higher-class gambling club in town. The Progressive opened in 1864. Chase later recalled, "The tables were the best Denver had known up to that time. The entire lower floor, 25 x 100 feet, was devoted to gambling, with the exception of the bar space. The second floor was also used by the fraternity, but in a more quiet way … " Denver's first billiard table, which had been transported across the prairie at the request of patron Jerome B. Chaffee, also shared the second floor.

Chase relocated briefly to Cheyenne, Wyoming, when it looked as though the railroad would bypass Denver completely. Upon returning he opened another establishment, the Cricket Hall, which offered everything from freak shows to music, gambling, and dime drinks. When Hub Healey died in 1870, Chase promoted his head bartender, Ed Gaylord, to full partnership. The Palace Variety Theater became another Chase enterprise, patronized by the rich (silver king Horace Tabor), the powerful (future senators Thomas Bowen and Edward Wolcott), and the soon-to-be-famous (journalist Eugene Field). Performers included national celebrities such as Eddie Foy, Lottie Rogers, and the Barbour Sisters, Addie and Frances Minerva. Frances would become the third (and last) Mrs. Ed Chase.

In his younger days, Ed had been notorious for his exploits with women. According to Robert K. DeArment in *Knights of the Green Cloth*, Chase's first marriage ended when his wife, Margaret Jane, stormed into the Corn Exchange gaming hall dressed as a man. She subsequently attempted to shoot a waitress named Nellie Bellmont, whom she accused of being Ed's mistress. After Margaret Jane sued for divorce, Ed Chase got married again, but not to the nefarious Nellie. His second marriage ended when he discovered that his beautiful wife, Helen, had been having an affair with a cattleman named George Brown. Helen disapproved of Chase's gambling enterprises and went looking for love in the wrong place when she could not force him into a career change. Ed followed Brown to Cheyenne, but when he took a shot at the rancher, the sheriff gave him a beating and tossed him in jail. Upon his release, Ed returned to Denver looking for Helen, who had wisely left town. When she divorced him, Chase did not contest. Helen moved to Omaha and eventually married Brown, who had prominent connections with the Nebraska Cattle Growers Association. Ed heard nothing more about Helen until twenty-six years later, when a newspaper contacted him for an interview. Apparently Helen had been placed in a mental institution by relatives after Brown's death.

In 1880, Ed Chase married twenty-year-old Frances Barbour, a charming young actress from Pennsylvania who had performed at the Palace Theater. Despite the twenty-three-year age difference, the couple remained happily married for life. Two years later, Chase's partner, Ed Gaylord, wed Frances's sister, Addie, in an elaborate wedding reported by the *Rocky Mountain News*.

Chase opened his most opulent gaming establishment in partnership with underworld kingpin Vasco Chucovich. Located across from the Brown Palace Hotel on Tremont Street, the handsome Italianate building opened in 1879 as Brinker's Collegiate Institute. Chase and Chucovich renamed the enterprise the Navarre, an opulent gambling hall that sported red velvet carpet and draperies and a white and crystal bar that was the envy of every saloon keeper in town. The apartments on the third and fourth floors were available for illicit liaisons, should the customers be so inclined. According to rumor, a tunnel connected the

Navarre with the Brown Palace so that patrons might travel secretly between the two buildings.

Chase's last gaming venture, the Inter-Ocean, combined a saloon, dance hall, and gambling house located at 1422 Curtis Street, the site of the old telephone exchange building. Decorated with Oriental rugs and exotic furniture, the mansion featured a maze of rooms and hallways that made for an easy escape in case of a raid. Regarding the odds at the Inter-Ocean, Ed once said in an interview that "All the chances are with the man who owns the house ... I thought they [the customers] might as well lose to me as to someone else, and I did the best I could to accommodate them."

Although Ed's actual date of retirement is in question, he was definitely out of business by 1916, when Denver went dry. He and Frances had lived at 2850 Lawrence Street for years, but later built a house at 1492 Race Street (eventually the site of the Aladdin Theater), where they entertained their many friends and business associates. When Ed died on September 27, 1921, Denverites were amazed to discover that his vast fortune had been reduced to $650,000.

According to his counsel, Mary Lathrop (Denver's first female lawyer), Chase had given away enormous sums over the years to broken-down gamblers and others in need. And despite his successful investments in real estate and public utilities, he had high overhead. Early in his career he dabbled in politics in an attempt to influence government officials and even served as an alderman during the 1860s.

In 1890, he became president of the Colorado Policy Association, something akin to today's Colorado State Lottery Board. Still, considerable sums were necessary to bribe police and other public officials. Ed also gave generously to friendly political candidates and helped stage the victory of Mayor Robert Speer in the notoriously crooked election of 1904.

Frances never remarried after Ed's death and remained in their home on Race Street until she passed away in 1946. The couple's only child had died in infancy, a boy named after Ed's brother John. In 1931, Frances adopted Addie's son, Gaylord Richard Snow, after his mother and stepfather moved to Panama. The young man elected to remain with his aunt in the United States and finish his education.

# THE TRINIDAD MADAMS'
## ASSOCIATION

Trinidad took a more enlightened approach to prostitution than many Colorado mining towns, possibly because the red-light district provided nearly 15 percent of the city's revenue. Since the Colorado Coal and Iron Company had outlawed bawdy houses and saloons in the coal camps, the town provided the closest outlet for love-starved miners looking for a good time. When Trinidad's madams banded together to form the Madams' Association, they wielded some serious political clout.

Their first accomplishment involved a creative marketing plan that brought customers right to their doorstep. Through a series of negotiations, the ladies arranged for direct access to the red-light district via a rerouted trolley line that would begin at the Jansen junction, where lines from the various mining camps conjoined. The Madams' Association financed construction of a bridge directly from the trolley junction to the red-light district, while the trolley company agreed to use the line for several years. When the company reneged on the agreement in 1922, the Madams' Association sued and won an out-of-court settlement.

Led by Trinidad madam Mae Phelps sometime around 1927, the ladies also built and maintained a madams' rest home. Located less than fifteen minutes from the trolley line at the west end of town, the foursquare brick house provided a safe haven for girls looking for a temporary escape or a much-needed vacation. Before the rest home was built, madams would send their drooping denizens to stay with local ranchers for a short time. According to historian Joanne Dodds, this arrangement caused problems for one newly married man named Thompson.

While driving to the ranch with his eastern bride, the cattleman received an exceptionally warm greeting from one of the prostitutes staying on his land. Before the rancher had the opportunity to introduce his wife, the prostitute assumed that Mrs. Thompson was "one of the girls," and made a few indelicate comments. Although the bride initially demanded a return ticket back home, the rancher convinced her to stay and the marriage survived.

### CHAPTER III

# Scandals and Triangles

### ❧

## Making the Front Page
*Hattie Sancomb and William Newton Byers*

*Rocky Mountain News* publisher William Newton Byers would have been the state's first governor had his former mistress not attempted to shoot him just before the Republican nominating convention. It was a pity, too. If anyone deserved to be governor, William Newton Byers had certainly earned the distinction. Smitten by gold fever in 1859, the young adventurer headed west from Omaha to the Cherry Creek goldfields, hauling a sturdy old Imperial printing press by oxcart through the Great American Desert. He published Denver's first newspaper, the *Rocky Mountain News*, on April 23, 1859, beating out his closest rival by several hours. Byers loved Denver and became the eternal booster, using the newspaper to tout the city and attract eastern investors, capital, and immigrants. (The enthusiastic editor sometimes got carried away. He once ran an advertisement intimating that the city could be accessed by steamboat.) Along with former governor John Evans, Byers created the Denver Board of Trade to promote construction of the Denver Pacific Railway, which secured the city's position as the rail hub of the Rockies. Without the enthusiastic Byers, Denver might well have faced oblivion or remained a dusty little settlement in the middle of nowhere.

A moderate man not given to drinking, carousing, or romantic flings, Byers had never been susceptible to the charms of women like Hattie Sancomb. Historian Robert L. Perkin speculates in *The First Hundred Years*, a history of the *Rocky Mountain News*, that at the time the editor "had just entered the roaring forties of his life, an age when men sometimes make a last rebellion against time and yearn nostalgically for young goathood." Perkin tries to defend Byers, intimating that "Lib [Elizabeth] Byers had developed into something of a shrew, pretentiously pious and away much of the time on grand tours with social climbing overtones." Since Mrs. Byers held a well-deserved position in the community something akin to sainthood, the criticism seems unfair.

More to the point, one admiring reporter gave the following description of mistress Hattie during her brief stint in court after shooting Byers: "She sat demurely in the courtroom with eyes of coal gray tint, regular features, dazzling teeth, penciled eyebrows, small poised head and wavy auburn hair. Her voice was soft and her manner caressing." Unfortunately, no photographs of the young woman remain to validate this enthusiastic report.

William Newton Byers and his wife, Elizabeth, might have been
Colorado's first gubernatorial couple had it not been for a pistol-wielding
redhead named Hattie Sancomb. *(Courtesy of the Denver Public Library,*
*Western History Collection, #Z-2349 and #Z-2339)*

The Byers-Sancomb affair began around 1871, while the
illustrious editor was serving as head of the Board of
Immigration, a nineteenth-century chamber of commerce.
Byers received a letter from a Mrs. Hattie E. Sancomb, a
milliner from Lawrence, Kansas, who asked about the business
opportunities in the Colorado Territory. A born promoter,
Byers painted a rosy picture and encouraged her to "Come on
out!" The beautiful divorcée stopped briefly in Denver to
thank Byers for his assistance, then moved on to Golden City.
Rival newspapers later claimed that he subsequently took on
her household expenses.

Hattie had many male admirers, but she set her cap, so
to speak, on Mr. Byers. After a brief exchange of intimate
notes (Byers later claimed that she pursued him relentlessly),

their friendship blossomed. They remained chummy through-out 1872 and 1873. By early 1875, it looked as though Colorado would finally achieve statehood, and Byers realized that the affair had to end if he wanted to become governor. Since Hattie had been pushing him to leave Elizabeth and the family, it must have seemed a good time to get out.

Mrs. Sancomb did not take rejection well. She stalked him for nearly a year, writing threatening letters, begging him to reconsider, and generally making a nuisance of herself. She even visited his home in January 1876, making his wife fully aware of their relationship. On March 31, she tried to storm into his office, but she couldn't get past the secretarial block-ade. Byers later said, "She sat there all day, alternately threatening, crying, and coaxing the employees to get to see me. She finally left in the evening, but returned again on Saturday morning, when the business manager was com-pelled to put her out." Apparently she drew her pistol and threatened to shoot, which should have given Byers a clue that she meant business.

On April 5, 1876, Hattie waited for Byers in the street after another unsuccessful assault on his office. When he got on the horsecar to go home for lunch, she ran alongside and tried to jump on. When driver finally stopped to let her aboard, she sat down on Byers's lap. The editor pushed her away and they both got off the trolley near the Byers home. As they quarreled, Hattie drew a pearl-handled pistol. Byers temporarily gained the advantage and pinned her arms behind her back.

Elizabeth Byers had witnessed the struggle from her window and hopped on her buggy, which happened to be standing near the door. As his wife galloped to the rescue, Byers released Hattie and jumped in the buggy with Elizabeth. Hattie then fired a shot that passed behind the seat, barely missing a little boy in the street. "In the excitement, the driving lines got caught in the single tree, so that the horse made a complete circle around where this woman was standing pistol in hand," Byers said later. "When within a few feet of me she attempted to fire a second time, but the pistol did not go off. We drove to the house and she followed, but my son, taking in the situation, stopped her at the gate with a revolver. I drove the horse to the stable and my wife went through the house and opened the front door, where her pistol got entangled in the sleeve of her dress and went off merely by accident." (The bullet barely missed Byers. Perhaps Elizabeth unconsciously took a shot at her errant spouse, understandable under the circumstances.) The police apprehended Hattie a few blocks away.

Although the Denver press did not report the shooting, the *Golden Transcript* broke the story on April 15, gleefully publishing Byers's love letters to Hattie. The editor, George West, admired Hattie and had at one time been employed by Byers. Naturally, Denverites vocally sided with the wronged wife, a pillar of the community, lady bountiful to the poor, leading clubwoman, and so on. On the other hand, men who had once thought Byers a sanctimonious bore began to look upon him more favorably, an opinion they wisely kept from their wives.

Byers's version of the story ran in the *Rocky Mountain Herald*, along with snippets from Hattie's more recent letters. "You've made me hate you again with all the deadly hatred a woman can have for a man, and you have always lied like hell to me, expecting to 'put me off.' Damn you, I will kill you!" When the news came out that Hattie's ex-husband, a Colonel Burns, had divorced her for adultery back in Kansas, the *Herald* labeled her "a damaged article" who had sought to take advantage of the hapless editor. Byers even accused Hattie of attempted blackmail, although he never presented any evidence.

When Hattie finally came to trial, the judge discreetly allowed the case to die on the docket. According to an 1881 newspaper article, Hattie went back to work as a milliner, in Golden. Byers gave up politics, although he continued to serve the city in numerous capacities and retained his position as a community leader. Mrs. Byers continued her charity work, although she spent more time at home and usually restricted her absences to occasions when she could travel in the company of her husband.

## ABOUT FACES

Throughout most of the nineteenth century, the ideal American woman had perfectly symmetrical features, a dainty Cupid's bow mouth, rosy blush, and a creamy white complexion (with bluish undertones if her corset was too tight). Since nature rarely bestowed flawless lily-white skin on the average female, this prerequisite for goddess-hood (like the eighteen-inch waist) presented a problem. In ranching and farming communities, women spent much of their time outdoors, acquiring unwanted suntans, dry skin, and wrinkles. Redheads fought freckles, teenagers fretted about acne, and smallpox victims suffered embarrassment due to scars or deep pits. Others who fell short of the standard included African Americans, Asians, Hispanics, Native Americans, and southern Europeans.

Although products that claimed to lighten the skin met with considerable interest, Victorians generally considered "face painting" the province of prostitutes. Men were often the staunchest critics of the rouged and powdered, possibly because they found it easier to distinguish sporting gals from "good girls" by their use of makeup. One cranky legislator tried to make it a misdemeanor for a woman under the age of forty-four to wear cosmetics, but fortunately his peers were reluctant to push their luck. Meanwhile, physicians, preachers, and publications continually assured young ladies that true beauty came from the heart.

In the February 1904 *Ladies Home Journal* columnist Carolyn Halstead took a poll of one hundred bachelors to determine which qualities they considered most important when choosing a wife. The gentlemen overwhelming favored (or so they said) "a domestic tendency," followed by love, a good disposition, and sympathy. Intelligence came in seventh, while beauty was rarely mentioned. Interestingly, the same publication sported several advertisements with pretty young girls hawking face powder.

Rather than use makeup, women were advised to attain a fresh glow (along with possible pneumonia) by taking a freezing bath in the morning. Less drastic suggestions included bathing the face in May dew or rainwater or applying a homemade beauty mask with ingredients such as honey, wheat germ oil, aloe, and comfy. Some magazines advocated mixing chalk powder and glycerin with cold water, and rubbing until skin became raw—a painful version of modern exfoliates. Others advised the reader to eat fresh vegetables and fruit or to rub her face with the juices, particularly of cucumbers. Homemade concoctions passed down through generations usually included herbs and natural ingredients such as buttermilk or almond meal. Western women used ground powder made of rice, chalk, or starch for whitening and sun protection.

Druggists became early dispensers of cold creams, which were generally harmless. Some creams have been around since the early 1900s, including Nivea, Noxema (which also treated sunburn and eczema), and Jergens lotion. Face whiteners, enamel, and "washes," on the other hand, could be lethal, since they were often laced with toxic ingredients, including mercury and lead. Some "experts" recommended eating arsenic wafers, which produced pallor by reducing oxygen to the blood. Unscrupulous traveling salesmen peddled the cheaper and more dangerous remedies in farming and frontier communities. Fortunately, the sale of poisonous products was curtailed somewhat after Congress passed the Pure Food and Drugs Act of 1906.

The advent of electricity in the 1880s may have spurred the gradual acceptance of face makeup, since the glow of a naked lightbulb is far less flattering than candlelight or gaslight. Women looked to professional beauties and actresses like Lily Langtree and Ethel Barrymore, emulating their idols by adopting stage makeup for evenings. By 1897, simple items such as rouge, eyebrow pencil, and face powder could be obtained through the Sears catalog, although some women were still embarrassed to make purchases. Attitudes about makeup changed perceptibly after World War I, as the flamboyant flapper replaced the Gibson girl, allowing entrepreneurs Elizabeth Arden, Helena Rubenstein, Madam C. J. Walker, and others to launch the modern cosmetics industry.

### ❦

# The Queen of Diamonds and the Jack of Hearts

*Louise Hill and Bulkeley Wells*

Of the many wheeler-dealers who struck it rich and subsequently lost their shirts during Colorado's gilded age, one of the most flamboyant was a mining engineer named Bulkeley Wells. Dashing, charming, and reckless, he had a way with women that catapulted him into the world of the rich and privileged. Unfortunately, he also had a romantic streak that proved fatal when he pushed his luck and his ladies a little too far.

One of Bulkeley's early conquests was Grace Livermore, a Boston socialite who just happened to be the daughter of a millionaire lawyer and mine owner. Her father, Col. Thomas Livermore, had invested successfully in several lucrative western mining properties, among them the Smuggler-Union, Telluride's richest mine. Bulkeley's career took a noticeable upward swing when he married Grace, and soon he was consulting on the national circuit as an expert in mineral engineering.

Colonel Livermore, who never quite trusted Wells, appointed him manager of the Smuggler-Union in 1902. The promotion was a dubious honor since Bulkeley's predecessor had moved on to that great gold mine in the sky, assassinated after a dispute with the local union. Unrest prevailed at the mine, where workers were poorly paid for long, dangerous hours underground. Under Bulkeley's management, mill and mine workers went on strike, demanding an eight-hour day and a minimum daily wage of $3. Gov. James H. Peabody sent in the National Guard and put Capt. Bulkeley Wells in charge, despite his direct involvement in the dispute. The appointment could hardly be called the act of an impartial government.

With the odds strongly in favor of management, Bulkeley broke the strike, rounded up union men and sympathizers, and booted them out of town. While the victory made him a hero in some circles, the Western Federation of Miners despised him. In 1908, someone placed a time bomb under his bed, happily on an evening when he had chosen to sleep out on the porch. The impact blew away the side of the house and sent him flying across the yard, but miraculously he escaped unharmed. Impressed, Colonel Livermore gave his son-in-law a less dangerous desk job as president of the Smuggler-Union.

Bulkeley's lucky streak continued when he met multimillionaire Harry Payne Whitney at an exclusive men's club in New York. Wells's bravado at the gaming tables so impressed Whitney that the pair formed a mining partnership, which put Harry's fortune along with the Livermore millions in the palm of Bulkeley's high-rolling hand. Wells expanded his operations from Mexico to Canada, taking big chances along the way. Besides presiding over the Smuggler-Union, which produced $50 million between 1902 and 1923, he headed up at least sixty other western mining companies. He invested millions in shaky ventures, including rejuvenation of the defunct Comstock Mine in Virginia City. Although he lost

Society queen Louise Hill hung her lover's portrait in the foyer of her Sherman Street mansion, next to a much smaller picture of her husband. *(Courtesy of the Denver Public Library, Western History Collection, #F-25956)*

more than he won, he stayed in the good graces of backers until he tangled with the queen of Denver society, Mary Louise Bethel Sneed Hill.

Mrs. Hill was a smoldering southern belle from Memphis married to Crawford Hill, who just happened to be the son of smelter magnate and U.S. senator Nathaniel P. Hill. Glamorous and ambitious, the older Louise snagged Crawford while he was still gullible and naive, a condition from which he never fully recovered. In 1900, the quiet and ultraconservative Crawford inherited his father's vast fortune and his business, which included the *Denver Republican* newspaper. Louise used the paper and the Hill millions to forge her own career as the city's social leader, malleting Denver's stodgy social set into a more acceptable reflection of sophisticated East Coast counterparts.

Although the city's "old guard" disapproved, Louise's talent for entertaining made her the most popular hostess in town. Instead of sipping tea and discussing fashions, children, and charity work, Louise held lively afternoon soirees for her friends. Businessmen from the 17th Street financial district joined in the fun, and Louise hired an instructor from New York City to give lessons on the finer points of modern dances. By 1913, Louise had outclassed all rivals, including her envious sisters-in-law, who left town. Denver's social calendar soon organized around her activities. The first harbinger of spring became the annual unveiling of a small nude female statue called "The Seasons," which graced the manicured gardens of her Sherman Street palace.

Louise Hill took her responsibilities as Denver's social lioness quite seriously. With a quick intellect and a personality dripping with southern charm, she might have been a diplomat had she been born a century later. A world traveler with political connections, she inveigled a formal presentation to King Edward VII of England as the unofficial goodwill ambassador for socially ambitious young Denver. In 1911, she literally rolled out the red carpet for President William Taft during one of his Colorado visits, extravagantly decorating the Hill estate with a vermilion walkway flanked by a forest of trees and shrubbery. Although she spent most of her time in Denver, she also entertained from an elegant New York City apartment and a rented Vanderbilt mansion in Newport Beach.

Louise became the best-dressed woman in the city—or at least the most expensively attired. A petite brunette with gray eyes, she wore only black or white, and her ensemble usually included an elaborate hat. She preferred diamonds and always wore or carried her trademark Easter lilies, draping them over everything, including her husband's casket. Details about her outfits, parties, and social activities were related to an adoring public ad nauseam by the city's newspapers, whose favor she courted with gifts to reporters.

"The Sacred 36" became the moniker for Louise's closed circle of friends, so named because they often got together for nine tables of cards at the Hill estate. At one point, she complained that there were only eighteen suitable people she could invite to dinners without recruiting from Colorado

Springs. She could make or break anyone with social aspirations, sinking unfortunates like Molly Brown before they ever got a toehold on the social ladder.

Louise and Bulkeley met sometime in the early 1900s, two rising stars destined to collide.

The Hills shared mutual mining interests with Wells, but Louise's interest in Bulkeley went far beyond stocks and bonds. The two began a remarkably open affair that lasted for years, despite the fact that both were married. Some cynical observers noted that the duo made adultery fashionable for the sophisticated woman, although most followed her lead more discreetly. In her foyer, Louise proudly displayed a large portrait of Bulkeley in tight polo trousers next to a much smaller picture of her husband, who never seemed to notice.

Although Bulkeley and Grace lived in Colorado Springs, Wells had an apartment in Denver. The gang at the country club often noticed Bulkeley and Louise leaving the dance floor together during social events or disappearing for extended periods. The laughing couple traipsed around town in Louise's elegant carriage, driven by an immaculately attired coachman and drawn by two sleek black horses. When the lovebirds traveled and dined together, the good-natured Crawford often tagged along, and the two men reportedly had a cordial relationship. A ménage à trois is possible but unlikely considering Crawford's personality.

In 1918, Grace Wells finally gave up in disgust. Tired of Bulkeley's frequent absences from the family nest, she filed for divorce on the grounds of desertion, retaining custody of their four children. Grace's father, Colonel Livermore, promptly withdrew his financial support and forced Bulkeley to resign as president of the Smuggler-Union. In 1921, Wells moved his main office to San Francisco. He and Louise kept in touch.

When fifty-seven-year-old Crawford Hill died in December 1922 after a long illness, Denver society expected Bulkeley and Louise to make a belated dash for the altar. Just three weeks after Crawford Hill's demise, Bulkeley Wells shocked everyone—especially his sixty-ish former mistress— by marrying a spicy twenty-three-year-old strawberry blonde named Virginia Schmidt. Since Mrs. Hill had just inherited millions and Virginia came from a middle-class family, this turned out to be an unwise financial move on Bulkeley's part. Infuriated, Louise ended their relationship and withdrew all financial support from her former paramour, convincing Harry Payne Whitney to do the same. Financially crippled, Wells hung on for eight more years, but the days of wine and lilies were obviously over.

Had he lived more carefully, Bulkeley's investments would have provided for a comfortable if not affluent old age. Instead he gambled heavily, both at the tables and in oil and gas speculations, and he lost it all. On the foggy San Francisco morning of May 26, 1931, he put a bullet in his head at age fifty-nine. Ironically, he never knew that representatives from the Western Pacific Railroad were waiting outside in the lobby, prepared to offer him an executive position paying $30,000 a year. Many old friends sympathized with his financial difficulties and mourned his loss. They also knew Louise well enough to understand why he chose to marry Virginia instead.

Louise never again spoke of her former paramour. During a cocktail party, *Rocky Mountain News* photographer Harry Rhodes once asked the socialite, "Do you know whatever became of Bulkeley Wells, Mrs. Hill?" À la Scarlett O'Hara, she smiled innocently and replied, "Why, I really don't know."

Mrs. Hill retained both her celebrity and her fortune through the Great Depression and the New Deal years, reigning for decades as the queen of Denver society. Her two sons, Nathaniel P. and Crawford, were educated back East and moved to New York City after their father's death. Louise's son Crawford did the family proud by marrying Elinor Dorrence, heiress to the Campbell Soup Company fortune.

As World War II broke out, the Sherman Street mansion became too expensive to maintain, even for a woman worth millions. After a slight stroke and a fall resulting in a broken shoulder, Louise moved into a luxurious suite at the Brown Palace Hotel in 1942. Five years later, the Jewish Town Club bought the Hill estate for $60,000. Since Louise had a cash-flow problem, her precious belongings, including a chandelier from Monticello, were auctioned off for well below their actual value. The elegant velvet cape she wore at King Edward's court sold for $22.50 and the famous "Seasons" statue for only $10.

Louise spent her last years in seclusion at the Brown Palace, pampered by a large staff of servants and nurses. She finally died of a stroke in 1955, at age ninety-five.

❧

# FLOWERSPEAK

Although flowers have long held religious or mythological significance, Victorians elevated their symbolic use to an art form. Instruction manuals for nineteenth-century courting couples usually devoted at least a chapter to the subject of floriography, which attached special meaning to every flower. Although the message might vary slightly depending on the book, complex sentiments could be attached to floral arrangements without the inconvenience of a paper trail if things didn't work out.

For example, the blossoming tuberose signaled an invitation to forbidden pleasures, while the number of leaves on its branch might mark the date and time of a secret assignation.

The color and petal arrangement of the flower also could change the meaning. Thus a white rose stood for silence, a yellow rose for jealousy. A red rose from a gentleman always meant, "I love you," while a daisy from the lady (symbolizing innocence) answered, "I'll think about it." (Unless of course she sent a double daisy, which meant "Let's go for it!") An ivy geranium politely asked, "Let's dance," while a yellow carnation demurred, "No, thanks."

A man could convey his feelings by sending the perfect bouquet to his sweetheart the morning after their date. An optimistic lover might present snowdrops, primrose, or iris decorated with baby's breath for sincerity or peppermint for warmth of feeling. If he wished to apologize for some transgression, he could send a bouquet of field lilacs for humility, brambles for remorse, or marigolds for sorrow. He was in real trouble if he received a striped carnation, which declared "This relationship is *so* over!"

A suitor might also present his love with a tussy mussy made of pewter, cobalt, glass, silver, or gold and filled with small clusters of flowers. The young woman could carry it as a fragrant addition to her outfit and bury her nose in it to quell the occasional stench of the horse-and-buggy era.

### ❧
# W. B. Daniels
# and the West Indies Witch
*"Donna Madixxa" and William B. Daniels*

*L*ilian Abbott swept into town like a West Indies hurri-
cane, leaving every man in her path sprawled helpless at
her feet. Tall and voluptuous with creamy olive skin and
raven hair, she had a classic beauty and gentility that veiled a
tempestuous and occasionally unstable personality. When the
young actress/teacher set out to charm aging department
store magnate William B. Daniels, the misguided millionaire
believed he'd found true love. Unfortunately, he soon discovered that life with Lilian could be exhausting. As Denver
newspapers reported unabridged details of their bitter part-
ings and passionate reconciliations, local gossips shook their
heads in disgust. Obviously, the old saw applied—there really
is no fool like an old fool, particularly a rich one.

Lilian had an unusual background. The Madrid-born
granddaughter of a Spanish count, she was christened Lilian
Donna Beardsley, but called herself "Donna Madixxa" on stage.
She also signed her name Lilian Beardslee or Lilyon Smith,
when the mood struck. Her royal blood came through her
mother, Maria Josefa Maguil, the daughter of Spanish Count
Madixxa and wife of a prosperous Connecticut merchant

named Beardsley. When Lilian turned seven the family moved to the West Indies, then relocated to Calistoga, California, six years later. The oldest of four children, she graduated from the Boston School of Oratory shortly before her father died. Since his death left her mother and siblings with no income, Lilian helped to support the family by teaching elocution until she could snare a husband, a grain commission merchant from Salem named Jonathan Abbott. Accustomed to high living, she spent lavishly, which put a strain on the brief marriage and nearly drove Abbott into bankruptcy. Lilian received no alimony in the divorce settlement, so after their parting, the twenty-eight-year-old joined her sister, Christine, and brother-in-law, George Hansel, in Denver, where both worked for the flourishing Daniels and Fisher Department Store.

Lilian immediately opened a school of elocution, tutoring about fifty students in public classes or private lessons. From the beginning she intrigued royalty-loving Denverites, who worshipped anyone with a title. In the first of many articles about Lilian, *The Rocky Mountain News* called her "a thorough teacher and a most charming and fascinating woman … Mrs. Abbott teaches not alone the use of the voice, but she teaches her pupils to breathe easily, properly and enough; to walk gracefully, to sit healthfully and elegantly, to gesticulate in a most artistic manner … " Lilian's statement in the same article sounds like a modern TV commercial: "Seven years ago I was an invalid and elocution made me what I am. I believe I have work to do in helping others

of my sex and showing them how to live. So few know how …"
Considering her future behavior, the good women of Denver
might have chosen a more restrained role model.

Among her clients, William B. Daniels gave her career
the greatest boost by obtaining a public endorsement for her
from fourteen of Colorado's most prominent citizens, including several Supreme Court judges, former governors, and
businessmen. Lilian had reportedly done wonders with
Daniels's son, William Cooke Daniels, a budding pyroma-
niac who once set fire to the Arapahoe Street Public School.
Although Willie had worse problems than poor diction, the
youngster became quite fond of Lilian and shared his father's
admiration for her innumerable talents.

By the autumn of 1881, widower William B. Daniels
was ripe for the plucking. Born in 1825, the former New
York farm boy began his career as a teacher. In 1855, a prominent Chicago merchant named Henry Potwin made the
young man a partner in an Iowa City, Iowa, clothing store,
which Daniels operated for eighteen years. Daniels's first wife
died early in their marriage, and in 1860 he married
Elizabeth, probably Potwin's daughter. He opened his first
Denver department store in 1864, under the name W. B.
Daniels & Co. Sometime around 1868, he recruited a new
partner named William Garrett Fisher. While Daniels took a
European jaunt for his health in 1875, Fisher built a new
department store on 16th and Lawrence Streets. Daniels
made his permanent home in Denver in 1879 and established another store in Leadville under the name Daniels,

Fisher and Smith. On June 22, 1881, his second wife died of tuberculosis, leaving him with an ornery ten-year-old son.

During a business trip to New York City that winter, Daniels frequently wrote to Lilian to inquire about Willie's progress. As the weather grew warmer (and their letters got hotter), rumors of an engagement spread. When Lilian canceled her elocution classes and took off for the East in June, Daniels followed. On July 8, 1882, they were married in Lyme, Connecticut, where William had placed his son in school. The wedding took place one year and sixteen days after the death of his first wife, allowing just enough time to muffle, if not silence, the gossips. Daniels began building a mansion for his new bride at 342 Curtis Street.

Within three months, the marriage began to fall apart. The couple quarreled about several matters, especially the housekeeper, Annie, who refused to obey Lilian's orders (possibly because she was also Daniels's mistress). Between William's stubbornness and Lilian's fiery temper, they were ready to separate by December 10. Hoping for a bit of peace and quiet, Daniels scheduled a business trip to Chicago. A repentant Lilian followed him to Union Station, boarded the train, and pleaded for another chance to work things out. Weary of his wife's theatrics, Daniels excused himself to go to the men's room and hopped off the train, leaving her stranded on the eastbound express. Infuriated, she wired her sister, Christine, for the money to get home.

As lawyers negotiated terms of a separation, the couple exchanged ardent love letters. Later published all over the country, his letters were signed "Pa Pa," Lilian's pet name for her balding spouse. Daniels wrote the first missive from New York, blaming their marital discord on Lilian's coldness and insistence that he fire poor Annie. In one of the more bizarre passages, he states, "I cannot tell you how miserable I have been since leaving you ... I was very nervous and could not have borne your repulses and neglect much longer. I want to give you $50,000 and take the legal separation, and it will not be three months before I will go to California for you and we will travel to our heart's content ... Of all the women in the world none are so supremely dear as my wife." The next day, "Pa Pa" wrote, "There is no woman in the world who has any attraction for me compared with my wife. There ought to be no doubt in your mind that we cannot live apart long ... I am bound in honor to get a legal separation or make myself appear ridiculous in the eyes of the public. After legal separation we can come together again with new love and affection ... "

Reluctantly, Lilian agreed to the separation and upped the ante to $75,000. After taking a fresh look at Pa Pa's million-dollar bankroll (he told her earlier that he had only $150,000), she decided that she wanted him back instead. According to their agreement, neither could visit the other without written permission, so Lilian coyly invited him to drop in and see her some time. "You can drive by the house in the sleigh and I can see how nice you look and I will throw you a sweet kiss from the window."

Daniels took the bait. "I will call at half past eight and if all is right, leave the lower part of the middle window blind partly open—of your chamber. Expect your husband at the time mentioned or as soon after the sign is given." Apparently crawling through the window for a late night tryst quickly lost its appeal, and two days later Daniels sent a brief note: "I have been to see the judge. He will fix up the papers and I can take you in my arms tonight and not have to walk a mile to sleep."

Although Lilian later claimed that they spent three nights together, the reconciliation never materialized and "Donna Madixxa" took off for New York to try her luck on stage. Gossips later hinted that Daniels's jealousy over a British capitalist named Lord Roquefort had factored into the final separation. Lilian eventually joined a traveling theatrical company and gained moderate success until the group played in Denver. When ecstatic fans greeted *la donna* and bombarded her with bouquets, the play's jealous leading man and lady quit the show in a huff. After the "Creole Company" went out of business, a droll *Rocky Mountain News* reviewer wrote, "'Article 47' will be seen no more at the opera house. The loss is not a very great one."

While in Denver, Lilian took the opportunity to file an alimony suit against Daniels, who had moved into the new Curtis Street mansion. When he tried to obtain a divorce on the grounds of adultery, Lilian bought a gun and sent the following note: "If such statements have been or shall be made by you or through your agency, as there is a God above I will kill you the first time I meet you." Understandably nonconfrontational, Daniels took the first train out of town. In a rage, Lilian stormed into the Curtis Street mansion waving the gun and barricaded herself in her husband's bedroom. A crowd of fascinated spectators watched as the police arrested her the following day for breaking and entering, carrying a concealed weapon, and inciting a riot. During a lively and widely publicized trial she pleaded innocent, maintaining that she and Daniels had an appointment, and that the threatening note had been forged. Oddly, the judge dismissed the case, determining that (a) one cannot break into one's own house; (b) no attempt was made to conceal the gun; and (c) by definition, a riot requires more than one person.

Lilian also won her alimony suit. Reaping the benefits of all that publicity, she returned to New York to star on Broadway in Agustin Daly productions. When she contracted spinal meningitis and became too ill to work, Daniels's attorneys offered her an additional $10,000 to agree to a divorce. Believing that she would only be charged with desertion, she finally gave in. On March 17, 1886, the courts granted Daniels a divorce on the grounds of adultery, which he never did prove.

Although Daniels paid Lilian's attorneys feels, court costs, temporary alimony, and a settlement of $85,000, she continually badgered him for more money. The aging playboy never got over the bad habit of seducing his employees and faced occasional lawsuits by angry husbands. Annie's spouse took him to court for alienation of affections, as did an African American employee whose wife worked in Daniels's Leadville store. Shortly afterward, Daniels's attorneys squelched rumors of his engagement to an unnamed blonde saleslady.

Over the next few years Lilian gained considerable weight, which effectively ended her stage career. After Daniels died in 1890, she filed an unsuccessful suit in the U.S. District court, claiming half of his estate as his rightful widow. She died of a heart attack a month after losing an appeal. Lilian's protégé, young Willie, fared much better. After inheriting his father's estate, young Daniels married into English royalty and on an international scale followed his father's lead as a playboy. In 1911, Willie also built one of Denver's favorite landmarks, the Daniels and Fisher tower. Fascinated by fire to the end, he requested cremation upon his death and directed that his ashes be placed in his father's store. During the 1960s, construction workers found an urn containing Willie's remains in the now-demolished Daniels and Fisher store. The urn and its contents now hold a place of honor in the D & F Tower, which has been renovated into an office complex.

# THE ALPHABET
# OF HIGH FASHION

From the ascension of Queen Victoria in 1837 until the aftermath
of World War I, women's fashions did everything possible to
exaggerate the female figure while hiding it under multiple layers
of clothing. During the early 1800s, the fashionable and more
fortunate woman wore a loose-fitting chemise with a high empire
waist, which made breathing and movement relatively easy. By
mid-century, her well-dressed counterpart resembled an inverted
letter *y*, with whalebone corsets constricting her middle and
voluminous skirts billowing out under wire hoops and crinolines.
Since the lady wore little or nothing underneath, a strong wind
could provide an intoxicating glimpse of ankle and possibly more.

After a slow start fifty years earlier, the bustle finally came
into its own in the early 1880s, accentuating the posterior and
changing a woman's shape into a lowercase *b*. By the early 1900s,
she looked more like an *s*, with jutting bosom and hips molded
into a swanlike configuration. In an era synonymous with
prudishness, women's clothing tickled the sexual imagination while
covering a lot of square footage.

In the best homes (and the finest parlor houses) ladies wore
rich fabrics such as brocaded velvet and silk in bold colors, with
plunging necklines for parties and evening wear. To produce the

ideal eighteen-inch waistline, the dreaded corset became the primary instrument of torture. Doctors weary of ministering to breathless females had condemned this engineering marvel, but it remained in vogue for nearly a century. Constructed of wire, canvas, and whalebone and padded with horsehair and stiff gauze, the corset could conceivably squeeze together muscle, bone, and cellulite to produce a waistline that a man could span with both hands. Although a few women had their lower ribs removed to achieve the right look, most suffered in silence and went easy on dessert. Before the padded bra, women could accentuate their bosom with a "pneumatic bust enhancer," or false breasts that were made of fine wire and woven into the desired shape.

Things were simpler for pioneer women. Ladies heading west in the late 1850s packed their good clothes in the trunk and wore simple, sturdy washable dresses of muslin or cotton with good buttons and trim. A cotton print called calico could be made into a relatively straight skirt with a lined bodice for extra strength and warmth. Corsets were laced very loosely, and hoops and crinolines were brought out only for special occasions. Her wedding dress became a woman's best outfit, made over two or three times as fashions changed. Bloomers, a sensible alternative to long skirts, never quite achieved the status of modern slacks or jeans.

Although ready-made garments became more easily available after the railroads steamed into Colorado in 1870, home sewing was still the rule. Parisian fashions could be copied from *Godey's Lady's Book* or *Ladies Home Journal.* The advent of the mail-order catalog revolutionized fashion for ambitious western women, bringing luxury as close as the nearest freight office. For the lady longing to breathe free, the 1880s saw the advent of the afternoon "tea gown," a soft garment with a loose waistline that could be worn without a corset. Styles changed rapidly between 1885 and 1900, issuing in the era of the tailored suit and frilly blouse with detachable collars and cuffs. Huge mutton sleeves began to lose popularity after 1893, possibly because they made the wearer look like a bird taking flight.

Although skirts rose a bit and clung more tightly after the turn of the century, women and their hemlines remained pretty much in place until World War I. As millions of young men registered for the draft, the girls back home considered it their patriotic duty to donate their corsets for scrap metal. Women breathed a sigh of relief when the brassiere hit the market around 1921. As the Roaring Twenties got into full swing, fashions reflected the changing values of a world turned upside down. The loose-fitting chemise with a shockingly short hemline came into vogue, providing the female form with a silhouette more closely akin to its natural outline.

### ✒

## Showdown
## at the Brown Palace Hotel
*Isabel and John Springer, Frank Henwood,*
*and Tony von Phul*

*T*he vamp of the Brown Palace Hotel, the infamous Isabel "Sassy" Springer, became the pivotal figure in a murder investigation on May 24, 1911, when two men fought to the death on her behalf. Sassy was married to a third gentleman at the time, an affluent cattle dealer named John W. Springer, who apparently spent too much time out on the range. Like a complicated Victorian morality play, the shooting of Tony von Phul by Frank Henwood ruined the lives of all participants, including two bystanders who just dropped by the Brown Palace bar for a drink.

The melodrama actually began in 1906, when widower John Springer met his future wife, Isabel, on a business trip to Saint Louis. A former lawyer from Illinois, the cattle baron owned considerable acreage in Highlands Ranch, now part of the southwest Denver metro area. Once listed among Denver's most prominent citizens, he made an unsuccessful mayoral bid in 1904, losing a rigged election to incumbent Robert Speer. That same year, Springer's wife, the former Elizabeth Clifton Hughes, died of tuberculosis, leaving him with a pre-adolescent daughter named Annie.

After two years in mourning, Springer fell in love with Isabel Patterson Folck, a divorced socialite twenty years his junior. The Saint Louis siren, nicknamed "Sassy," had several other admirers, which undoubtedly made her even more attractive to the graying cattleman. A brown-eyed beauty with an hourglass figure, she possessed all the qualities a man might desire in a woman, except perhaps common sense. The only male she failed to charm was Springer's business partner and former father-in-law, Col. William E. Hughes, who eyed the relationship suspiciously because of Isabel's reputation as a party girl.

Although John Springer must have been aware of Sassy's foibles, he married her anyway. Alarmed, Colonel Hughes withdrew from his business dealings with Springer in 1907 and used his influence to gain custody of Annie. After the initial infatuation wore off, Springer paid more attention to his racehorses than his trophy wife, which must have been irritating to a glamour girl like Sassy. Bored, she took advantage of their numerous trips to New York to experiment with alcohol and drugs. While her husband remained preoccupied with business dealings, she posed in the nude for artists and embraced a bohemian lifestyle. She later became addicted to opium, a cure-all for Victorian women when mixed with alcohol to form a "medication" called laudanum.

The Springers occupied three separate Colorado residences: a mansion in downtown Denver, a suite at the Brown

Socialite Isabel (Sassy) Springer figured prominently in
a love triangle and murder at the Brown Palace Hotel.
*(Courtesy of the Denver Public Library, Western
History Collection, #F-10178)*

Palace Hotel, and a ranch in Littleton. While at her home on
the range, Sassy probably began an affair with her husband's
business associate, the dapper but neurotic Harold Francis
(Frank) Henwood. Things got out of hand when Sassy's other
boyfriend, a traveling salesman named Sylvester (Tony) von
Phul, rolled into Denver, ostensibly to go hot air ballooning

over Pikes Peak. Obviously mad for the hunk she called "Tony Boy," Isabel had written passionate letters begging him to come to town ( " … all the love a woman is able to give, I am sending to you, the only man I have ever loved.") A big-time risk taker, she sometimes penned these juicy notes while her husband sat in the next room.

According to Dick Kreck in *Murder at the Brown Palace*, Tony and Sassy may have been lovers long before she married the more financially attractive Springer. Still besotted with von Phul, Sassy tried to lure him back by hinting at Henwood's attentions in her correspondence. The strategy backfired when a jealous von Phul threatened to show her love letters to Springer. With her future as a lady of leisure at stake, Sassy begged Frank Henwood (of all people) to retrieve the incriminating evidence. At Frank's insistence she reluctantly wrote a Dear John note to von Phul calling off their relationship, which the aeronaut received when checking into the Brown Palace. Since von Phul had come all the way from Saint Louis at Sassy's expressed invitation, he had good reason to doubt the letter's sincerity.

Despite the attempted blackmail and her faux good-bye, Isabel continued to rendezvous with Tony von Phul, which infuriated Frank Henwood. Perhaps she set her lovers against each other on purpose, hoping to rid herself of both. She may have enjoyed the ego boost, or perhaps the drama provided an outlet for frustrated theatrical aspirations. More likely, she had absolutely no idea what she was doing.

Now on a mission, Henwood asked the Denver police chief to force the newcomer out of town, supposedly in the interest of his friend Springer. When the official refused, Henwood stormed over to the Brown Palace to confront his rival. A serious athlete, Tony von Phul was not easily intimidated. He grabbed a shoe tree, bashed Frank over the head, and tossed him out at gunpoint.

Seething, Frank bought a pistol of his own. Ignoring Sassy's pleas to drop the matter, Frank Henwood accosted his adversary in the Brown Palace Mayfair Room after von Phul returned from an evening at the theater. Annoyed by his rival's antics, von Phul punched him in the face, but this time Frank had come prepared. He drew the gun and shot von Phul three times, then fired two bullets that went astray and injured two bystanders. After apologizing to the victims for his poor aim, Henwood stood stunned as an elevator operator grabbed the gun from his hand. A musician and future bandleader named Paul Whitman assisted the mortally wounded von Phul, who claimed that he had been unarmed. Tony von Phul passed away twelve hours later at Saint Luke's Hospital, followed by a second victim, George E. Copeland, who died in surgery. A third innocent party, James Atkinson, recovered after being shot in the leg, but remained disabled for life.

Although officials attempted to preserve Sassy's reputation, newspapers caught wind of her involvement and printed several of the incriminating love letters. Less than two weeks after the shooting, Springer filed for divorce. The swiftness of Denver justice became apparent just three weeks later, when authorities brought Henwood to trial for Copeland's murder. Eyewitness reports differed, but some testified that Henwood had fired on the unarmed von Phul after he turned his back. If von Phul did have a gun, it mysteriously disappeared from the scene. Subpoenaed to testify at the trial, Sassy gave a highly emotional account of events, dealing mostly with her attempts to stop Henwood. Frank positioned himself as a hero who should be congratulated for killing the ruffian who threatened his friend's marriage, obviously forgetting that he was really on trial for Copeland's death. The jury found Frank Henwood guilty of second-degree murder on June 29, 1911, and sentenced him to life imprisonment in Cañon City.

After Henwood filed several appeals, a higher court overturned his conviction on a technicality and ordered a second trial. This time the jury found him guilty of first-degree murder and ordered his execution. A forgiving Springer successfully intervened with the governor, who commuted the sentence back to life imprisonment. The cattleman showed less compassion toward Sassy, allowing her a minimal settlement if she promised to leave Denver and never return. The former beauty moved to New York City and occasionally found work as an actress and model, dying her hair white in a futile attempt to hide her identity. Drug and alcohol addiction destroyed her looks, and she died broke in a charity ward just six years after the shooting.

Henwood remained in prison until 1922, when Springer convinced the governor to grant clemency. Frank vowed to begin a new life in New Mexico, but landed back in prison within months after threatening to kill a woman who wouldn't marry him. He died in Cañon City in September 1929, maintaining until the end that his attack on Tony von Phul sprang from a sincere desire to protect the Springers' marriage.

In 1915, John Springer married another divorcée named Jeanette Lotave; like Sassy she was at least twenty years his junior. Although Springer tried to erase all evidence of his unfortunate second marriage, the scandal effectively destroyed his reputation and squelched any political aspirations. He limited public appearances and gradually sold off his property, experiencing financial losses along the way. Tragedy struck again several years later, when his daughter, Annie, committed suicide. John Springer died in 1945 and lies buried next to Jeanette in the Littleton Cemetery.

## ❧
# Lovestruck Ladies of
# Pitkin County
### *Clara Dietrich and Ora Chatfield*

*I*n July 1889, two young women from a prominent Colorado family made headlines when the press went public with details of their sensational love affair. The society of Pitkin County was "rent from center to circumference," according to the *Denver Times*, over the avowed passion between Clara Dietrich, a postmistress and storekeeper in her mid-twenties, and her cousin, Ora Chatfield, whose age lay somewhere between fifteen and seventeen. Both young women were nieces of wealthy rancher Isaac W. Chatfield, after whom both Chatfield Dam and Chatfield Park in Littleton were later named.

With relish disguised as shock, the *Times* related the scandalous details of the lesbian love affair:

A month or more ago, Ora Chatfield was suffering so from nervous prostration and the matter was investigated. It was ascertained that she was madly in love with Miss Dietrich, with whom she was living. The two were torn apart and a warrant was procured in Aspen for the arrest of the older with the intention to have an investigation made as to her sanity. She promised the sheriff with tears trickling down her cheek and her voice choking with suppressed emotion to give up her child wife.

Love letters written by the women before Dietrich's arrest convinced the sheriff that "the love that existed between the parties was of no ephemeral nature but as strong as that of a man for his sweetheart." Ora usually signed her letters to Clara "Hubby." With a giant leap of fancy, the *Times* continued, "If the case ever comes into court, from a scientific standpoint alone it will attract widespread attention and if elucidated it will perhaps explain some of the so-called occult sciences."

Matters came to a head a few days after Clara's arrest, when she traveled to Aspen with the "avowed intention" of marrying an unnamed gentleman who lived near Emma. Ora Chatfield also took a trip in the same direction, ostensibly to visit relatives. After a rendezvous in Aspen, the girls "eloped" to Denver together. Apparently the family asked I. W. Chatfield to find Ora and bring her back home, but the *Times* never reported his eventual success or failure.

For some unknown reason, the *Times* also interviewed an unidentified "prominent and influential citizen of Aspen," who had been visiting in Denver. "Both girls appear to be perfectly rational for everything but their unnatural affection for each other," the source observed. "Their reputations have always been above reproach and in all matters outside of this,

Miss Dietrich appears to be a very sensible girl." He described Dietrich as a tall blonde with a good figure and commanding presence, while Ora was slender with a delicate physique, "a remarkably handsome girl who would attract attention anywhere she went."

After a fruitless search for the women in Denver, the *Times* concluded that they were living in a hotel under assumed names or had already moved on to another location. Neither woman is listed in the family genealogy or buried in the family plot at Fairmount Cemetery.

# ❧
# The Unequal Wages of Sin
*Baby Doe Tabor and Arabella Huntington*

*A*lthough quite different in looks and personality, both Elizabeth McCourt (Baby Doe) Tabor and Arabella Huntington were exquisite as young women. While the flirtatious Baby Doe charmed admirers with her high spirits, full figure, golden curls, and sapphire-blue eyes, the more refined Arabella turned heads with a slender, statuesque form, dark hair, enormous brown eyes, and perfect features. Intelligent and ambitious ladies of dubious reputation, both snagged inordinately wealthy Gilded Age giants at least twenty-five years their senior. Since the gentlemen in question (silver king Horace Tabor and railroad baron Collis Huntington) were already married at the time, the ladies were paramours long before they became wives. Although Arabella made the transition from mistress to Mrs. without a social ripple, Baby Doe ignited a national scandal that still smolders more than a century later.

Baby Doe and Arabella followed a similar path up to a point, but their stories had drastically different endings. Arabella Huntington became a social empress and one of the country's richest women, respected, admired, and even feared in some quarters. An art collector of the highest order, she bequeathed to posterity two great cultural institutions, the Huntington Art Museum and the Huntington Library in southern California. A polar opposite, Baby Doe Tabor lost her fortune, her husband, and eventually her mind while still a relatively young woman. The former silver queen spent her final years alone in a mountain cabin near Leadville, where she froze to death in February 1935. As her legacy, Baby Doe left behind Colorado's favorite love story, an engrossing tale of passion and betrayal that is the stuff of grand opera and Greek tragedy.

### An Echo of Silver
### *The Story of Baby Doe Tabor*

The daughter of a prosperous Irish tailor and dry goods merchant, Elizabeth (Lizzie) Bonduel McCourt grew up in comfort if not luxury. As the prettiest girl in Oshkosh, Wisconsin, Lizzie liked to flaunt her assets, which made her popular among men but generally disliked by other women. She had an ample supply of suitors, including the dapper William H. (Harvey) Doe, son of an affluent local businessman. When the couple married in June 1877, their large wedding attracted a standing-room-only crowd. The newlyweds immediately headed for Colorado, where Harvey's father owned a half-interest in the Fourth of July Mine near Central City.

The mining venture failed soon after their arrival, as did most of Doe's endeavors. As successive enterprises soured, Lizzie realized that her irresponsible husband could never provide the lifestyle she wanted. Harvey drifted from job to job,

Both Baby Doe Tabor and Arabella Huntington romanced and wed much older multi-millionaires, but their stories ended quite differently. *(Baby Doe Tabor photo courtesy of the Colorado Historical Society, #F-737)* *(Arabella Huntington photo courtesy of the Huntington Library, #HEH61-2)*

their marriage collapsed, and the pair separated. Too pretty to be alone for long, Lizzie befriended a Jewish merchant named Jacob Sandelowsky (later changed to Sands), a twenty-eight-year-old bachelor who plied her with gifts and kept her in groceries. She frequently accompanied Jake to a raucous variety hall in Central City, where her peaches-and-cream complexion inspired miners to nickname her "Baby Doe."

When Jake moved to Leadville to open a new store, Baby Doe decided to shed Harvey for good. While her errant husband visited a Market Street brothel in Denver, she followed him and asked a policeman to serve divorce papers. In spring 1880, she joined Jake in Leadville. Their time together would be short, for she soon caught the wandering eye of silver king

Horace Tabor, Leadville's favorite celebrity. Before long she had her own suite in Leadville's Clarendon Hotel.

Tabor had barely turned fifty when he began keeping company with Baby Doe. A strong and relatively tall man for the times (five foot, ten inches), he had dark hair, a receding hairline, a walrus moustache, and a visionary gleam in his eye. With his wife and son, Tabor had left his Kansas farm in 1860 to prospect the California Gulch area near present-day Leadville. Like many early pioneers, the Tabors led a nomadic existence for the first few years, moving from Oro City to Buckskin Joe before finally settling in the new town of Leadville. Although Tabor never made a major strike on his own, he and his wife, Augusta, prospered as storekeepers. Wherever they went, the Tabors became involved with the community. Horace often served as postmaster or held minor political offices.

Gregarious and generous, Tabor extended credit to prospectors in return for a share of any profits. He generally lost money on these ventures until April 1878, when German immigrants August Rische and George Hook helped him parlay a modest investment into a bonanza with the Little Pittsburg silver mine. As Tabor's career as an entrepreneur took off, he became involved in speculative business enterprises around the state, wielding unrivaled economic power. He loved the high life and spread his millions freely, building grand hotels and opera houses in Leadville and Denver.

As Tabor's star rose, his relationship with Augusta faltered. After twenty hard years on the frontier, Augusta had lost her youthful good looks. A conservative New Englander

to the end, she disapproved of Tabor's indiscriminate spending and said so. Despite her sharp tongue, she loved him and
was badly hurt when he walked out in July 1880. The humil-
iation must have been unbearable when Tabor brought the
glamorous Baby Doe to Denver and installed her in luxurious
rooms at the Windsor Hotel. As one of the hotel's major
stockholders, he could provide numerous amenities for Baby's
elegantly furnished suite, which included a gold leaf bathtub,
marble fireplace, diamond-backed mirrors, and a hand carved
1,500-pound walnut bed.

Still, Augusta refused to give the silver king a divorce. To
rid himself of a bothersome wife, Tabor called upon his right-
hand man, William Bush. In a convoluted series of events,
Bush secured a divorce (which turned out to be illegal) in
Durango, where Tabor owned property. Perhaps unaware
that the action had been fraudulent, Tabor secretly married
Baby in Saint Louis on September 30, 1882. On January 1,
1883, the courts granted Augusta a legal divorce on the
grounds of desertion and nonsupport, providing her with a
$300,000 property settlement. In an emotional scene that
gained her much sympathy, she tearfully told the court that
the divorce was "not willingly asked for."

The gossip adversely affected Tabor's bid for the U.S.
Senate, a race that he lost by a slim margin to another mining baron, Thomas Bowen. As a political booby prize, Tabor
filled a one-month vacancy in the Senate that arose when
President Arthur appointed Senator Henry Teller to a cabinet post. Taking full advantage of his office, the thirty-day

congressman staged a lavish (and legal) wedding for Baby Doe, which was held in the Willard Hotel in Washington, D.C. Although the president and his cabinet attended the ceremony, their wives stayed home.

The Tabor triangle caused a national scandal. Horace and Baby Doe were labeled "vulgar" and publicly vilified, particularly after newspapers went public with the Saint Louis ceremony and Durango divorce fiasco. In Denver, they found themselves ostracized by the social set. While Horace could still function in business, the wives of his associates stood staunchly behind Augusta and ignored Baby Doe. Although the snub undoubtedly hurt, Horace and Baby Doe managed to live happily. They pampered and adored their two much-photographed daughters, Lily (born in 1884) and Silver Dollar (born in 1889). The Tabors gave generously to the community, investing heavily in Colorado's future. Baby Doe even provided space in the Tabor block on 16th Street for headquarters during the successful woman's suffrage campaign of 1893.

Although Horace's personal life improved, his financial situation deteriorated and he fell deeply into debt. Wild land speculation, numerous lawsuits, unprofitable mining investments, and the declining silver market seriously eroded his assets long before the 1893 Depression dethroned the silver kings. Although Tabor always had helped others, his so-called friends turned their backs and watched him go broke. Reduced to the level of a common laborer shoveling slag in Cripple Creek, he regained some of his old optimism after Sen. Edward Wolcott secured for him an 1898 appointment as Denver postmaster. Unfortunately, he died of appendicitis the following year. Baby Doe moved to a cabin near a storage shed at the Matchless Mine, where she spent the next thirty-five years living on charity. Despite the romantic fable, it's highly unlikely that Horace whispered to Baby Doe on his deathbed, "Hold on to the Matchless, it will make millions again." Both were aware that the mine had gone into fore-closure years earlier.

Baby Doe's final years were tragic. At eighteen, her old-est daughter, Lily, decided to live with McCourt relatives in Wisconsin and never returned. Silver Dollar (Honeymaid) wanted to be a writer and produced one very bad novel, *Star of Blood.* Sadly, she fell victim to drug and alcohol addiction and moved to Chicago, eventually descending into prostitu-tion. Silver died in 1925, scalded to death and possibly murdered in a cheap Chicago flophouse.

## Beating the System
### *Arabella Huntington*

Arabella Duval Yarrington Worsham Huntington had a gift for covering her tracks. Under the guidance of her wealthy benefac-tor, Collis Huntington, she moved from faro parlor to Fifth Avenue, climbing to the summit of the social ladder without a stumble. While the constant danger of discovery must have been troublesome, the gains obviously compensated for the risks.

Although Arabella's birth certificate has never been located, she may have been born in Alabama or Virginia some-time between 1847 and 1852, the daughter of a machinist and carpenter named Richard Yarrington. When Yarrington passed away in 1859, his wife, Catherine, took in boarders to help support their five children. While still in her teens, Arabella (whose real name might have been Eliza, Emma, or Carolina) became involved with Johnny Worsham, a gambler who ran a flashy faro parlor a few blocks from their home in Richmond, Virginia. When Union troops set fire to the city in 1865, Johnny and other members of the sporting fraternity wisely headed north. Arabella soon joined him in New York, with the entire Yarrington clan close on their heels.

According to Arabella, she married Johnny and shortly afterward gave birth to a son named Archer. The exchange of vows may have been one of Arabella's fabrications, since Worsham was married already to a woman in Richmond. For reasons unknown, Johnny went back to his legal wife in 1870, and Arabella told folks that he had died. During the "mourning period," the "widow Worsham" and her extended family moved into a beautiful new house in a fashionable neighborhood, purchased by Collis Potter Huntington, one of the country's wealthiest and most powerful tycoons.

The mastermind of the Central Pacific and Southern Pacific Railroads, Huntington began life modestly in 1821, near a swamp aptly named Poverty Hollow in Harwinton Township, Connecticut. One of nine children born to a struggling tinker, he left home at fifteen and eventually joined his older brother in the dry goods business. At twenty-three, he married Elizabeth Stoddard, a plump, innocuous young woman who remained so far in the background that many people never knew that she existed.

Huntington subsequently headed west during the California gold rush of 1849. A large man with the build of a lumberjack, he eventually joined forces with Leland Stanford, Mark Hopkins, and Charles Crocker to become the leader of California's "Big Four." Through fair means and foul (mostly foul), they created one of the world's most extensive railroad lines, becoming disgustingly rich in the process.

Exactly how Collis met Arabella remains a mystery, but they may have become acquainted while she still lived in Virginia. In 1877, the railroad baron subtly maneuvered the social introduction of his "niece," Mrs. B. D. Worsham, through an article in an Austin, Texas, newspaper. For the next several years Arabella would live a life of quiet respectability, educating herself in the arts and architecture while she renovated and redecorated her West 54th Street home and dabbled in real estate. Huntington's visits were so discreet that not a whisper of scandal ever touched the lovely widow, who always comported herself with propriety. Her mother or one of her sisters always accompanied Arabella when she went out.

Approximately nine months after Elizabeth Huntington's death in 1883, Arabella became the second Mrs. Collis Huntington. New York society never batted an eye, despite the age difference and their supposed familial relationship. The newlyweds built a grand mansion at 65 Park Avenue, and Arabella set about introducing her rugged husband to the arts.

For the next seventeen years, willing or otherwise, he took his new wife to the opera, to art auctions, and anywhere else she'd been waiting to go. When Collis died in 1900, he left Arabella $150 million, which translates to more than $4 billion in today's currency—a nifty retirement after thirty years of dalliance and marital bliss.

During the early 1900s, Mrs. Huntington traveled extensively abroad and entertained herself by snatching up the world's great art. In 1910, she gave up her Paris mansion and moved back to New York, sparking rumors that she would wed Collis's scholarly nephew, Henry E. Huntington, who had inherited one-third of his uncle's estate. As manager of Collis's California railroads, Henry had become very close to the tycoon. Arabella's son, Archer Worsham, was left out of the will completely. Although nuptials between the two Huntingtons might have been suspect in some quarters, Henry obviously worshipped Arabella, who was only a few years older than him and still retained her good looks at sixty (or so). Three years later in Paris, they consolidated the marriage/merger.

Henry loved books the way Arabella loved painting and sculpture, and the couple made acquisition of great literature and fine art the focus of their life together. Unlike Arabella, definitely a New York type of gal, Henry wanted to make his home in southern California. To entice his bride out West, he acquired enormous tracts of land near Los Angeles and built a fabulous mansion at his San Merino ranch. When he asked Arabella to oversee construction, she agreed to supervise the project completely—from a distance. The ploy having proved unsuccessful, Henry had to resign himself to brief annual visits to California. Although the Huntingtons dropped by only often enough to check on their budding museum and library, San Marino eventually became the repository for their impressive collections. Henry compiled the largest collection of great books ever owned by a single individual in the United States, while Arabella became one of the world's most astute art collectors. After she died in 1924 and Henry followed in 1927, the couple left $8 million for maintenance of two of California's great cultural treasures, the Huntington Museum and Library.

### CHAPTER IV

# *Lovers for Life*

🎀

## Love on a Merry-Go-Round
*Mary and John Elitch*

*I*n the late nineteenth century, amusement parks were as much a part of Denver's entertainment scene as theater, opera, or vaudeville. Elitch Gardens shared the scene with several other pleasure parks, including Riverfront Park, Manhattan Beach, Arlington (Chutes Park), Tuileries Gardens, and later White City, which became Lakeside. The grand era of amusement parks came to an end around World War I, although Elitch Gardens and Lakeside continued to entertain Denverites into the next century.

Despite pouring rain and muddy roads, Denverites flocked to the outskirts of the city on May 1, 1890, for the grand opening of Elitch Gardens. At the entrance, a handsome young couple named Mary and John Elitch welcomed the city's elite to a delightful new amusement park, hailed by local newspapers as "a milestone in the city's progress."

Modeled after the fabled Woodward Gardens in San Francisco, the park was the ultimate pleasure palace, shimmering with blossoming flowerbeds lined by walkways and sparkling fountains. On a grassy knoll under the cottonwoods, the strains of a waltz drifted from the band shell, while under a canvas tent, vaudeville performers delighted the audience with comedy and song. Shady picnic spots, a blossoming apple orchard, a lake for boating, and even a small zoo made Elitch Gardens the ideal spot for a family outing for generations to come.

Elitch's success was due partly to the popularity of Mary and John Elitch, who were Denver's golden couple at the time. "The Gracious Lady of the Gardens," as newspapers fondly called Mrs. Elitch, had the charm of a fairy-tale princess coupled with artistic flair and an enviable strength of character. Born Mary Elizabeth Hauck sometime around 1856, she was still a child when her family moved from Philadelphia to a prosperous farm and ranch in California. A lively, petite brunette with a broad (and sometimes mischievous) smile, she may have given her parents a few headaches before they sent her away to school at a Catholic convent. Their worst fears must have been realized when, at sixteen, she eloped against their wishes with a young man she had met in church. "He swept me off my feet," she later said of the groom, John Elitch Jr., a stage-struck twenty-two-year-old athlete with black curly hair and deep-blue eyes. A true romantic, he presented her with a beautiful leather bound copy of *The Rubaiyat of Omar Khayyam* as a wedding present. They spent their honeymoon

The delightful John and Mary Elitch founded Denver's most popular amusement park in 1890. *(Courtesy of the Elitch Library)*

in San Jose, where he took Mary to see her first play, *The Streets of New York*. Like her handsome husband, she was hooked on the theater forever.

John Elitch had big dreams. Born on April 10, 1850, in Mobile, Alabama, he came from an illustrious family that chose the wrong side during the Civil War. While still in his twenties, he moved to San Francisco and opened a restaurant in a local theater building. After investing the proceeds in an unsuccessful traveling vaudeville show, he relocated to Denver in 1880. John found work in the Arcade Restaurant at 16th and Larimer Streets and the following spring took off for Durango, the latest Colorado boomtown, to open a restaurant. Since the Rio Grande Railroad was still under construction, he and his employees had to walk part of the distance through the deep snows of the Conejos Mountain Range carrying a sheet-iron range and cooking equipment on their backs. Lacking real competition, John struck it rich, charging town promoters $1.50 for a porterhouse steak. With $4,000 in his pocket, he returned to San Francisco and lost everything in another theatrical venture.

Undaunted, John tried Denver again in the winter of 1881–82. With a friend's financial assistance, he opened an oyster- and chophouse with his father at 16th and Curtis Streets. The restaurant succeeded spectacularly, like all of John's culinary ventures. A terrific cook and caterer, he was clearing $1,000 a month (more than $20,000 today) when he decided to expand the business. In 1886, John and Mary opened a new restaurant at 1561 Arapahoe Street called Elitch's Palace. One of the finest dining establishments in town, it featured Mary's paintings and artwork, a huge kitchen, and even electricity. John's warm personality and winning ways soon made him the city's favorite caterer, and he numbered among his close friends poet and journalist Eugene Field, millionaire Horace Tabor, and showman P. T. Barnum. For his friends, Elitch created the Gout Club and helped organize the Denver Athletic Club, at one time serving as its president.

With the proceeds from his latest success, John considered investing in another traveling vaudeville show, but decided instead to open an amusement park that would include a theater. He began searching for a property with plenty of trees and good water rights, and in 1887 found the ideal spot, a sixteen-acre plot in north Denver called the Chilicott Farm. John purchased the property and presented Mary with a *fait accompli*. The couple developed their future pleasure palace with loving hands. John planted more hardwood trees and a vegetable garden for the park's restaurant, to be called the Orchard Café, while Mary installed new flowerbeds. They sold the restaurant, Elitch's Palace, in 1888 and opened the amusement park two years later.

Elitch Gardens quickly became a local favorite, typically attracting eight to ten thousand patrons on a Sunday. When the couple made $35,000 during the first season, John used part of the windfall to form another theatrical company. Amazingly, this enterprise actually proved profitable. Elitch, Schilling & Goodyear's Traveling Minstrels began a tour of major western cities, with plans to return to Denver for summer performances at the gardens. One of the members, a musical comedy star named Charles Schilling, later married Mary's sister, Anna.

During the final weeks of the tour, John fell ill. After playing two nights at the Alcazar Theater in San Francisco, he collapsed in a fever. Fellow performers carried him back to his hotel room and wired Mary, who caught the first train. She remained at John's bedside until he died three weeks later of pneumonia. With a broken heart, Mary buried the love of her life on March 11, 1891, at Fairmount Cemetery in Denver, arranging to have John's bas-relief portrait carved on the headstone. Rather than sell the amusement park, "I determined to make these gardens a memorial to my husband," she wrote.

Before summer she had completed work on the playhouse that had been John's dream, the Theater in the Gardens.

Elitch Gardens hosted numerous Denver "firsts," including the debut of Thomas Edison's Vitascope, a forerunner of motion pictures. A born theatrical promoter, Mary formed a summer stock company in 1897, choosing great directors and actors, including James O'Neill, father of famous playwright Eugene O'Neill. Many future Broadway and movie stars played Elitch Summer Theater, such as silent film hero Harold Loyd, Edward G. Robinson, Frederic March, and Cecil B. DeMille, who later dubbed Mary's theater "the cradle of the American drama." A later list of Elitch Theater players reads like the who's who of Hollywood, including Walter Pigeon, Ginger Rogers, Lana Turner, and Grace Kelly. Even the illustrious Sarah Bernhardt performed in 1906 after the great earthquake prevented her San Francisco appearance. Her leading man was the future silent film swashbuckler Douglas Fairbanks Sr., who had grown up in Denver and attended East High School.

An expanding zoo became the great Elitch Gardens attraction for youngsters. As the first female zookeeper in the world, Mary had a special way with critters large and small. "The best animal importers had standing orders from me to supply the Gardens with fine and rare specimens," she said in 1934. Her menagerie included two large black bears named Sam and Dewey, an albino buffalo, an elephant, and a racing ostrich trained to the harness. Another favorite pet, a lioness named Gladys, had been bottle-fed by Mary as a cub. Mellow and friendly as a kitten (or so Mary said), Gladys rode in a float during the 1896 Festival of Mountain and Plain.

Mary always loved youngsters, although she never had any of her own. As a writer of children's stories she became an honored member of the Denver Woman's Press Club, where her large portrait still hangs in a place of honor. She added many attractions to Elitch Gardens specifically for children, including the diminutive steam engine that toddled around the property, the musical merry-go-round, and the Toboggan Coaster Ride. Mary held costume parties and contests, provided painting, dancing, and dramatics lessons, and led nature walks and sing-alongs. On Tuesdays, children were admitted free.

In November 1900, the Gracious Lady of the Gardens wed her longtime assistant, Thomas D. Long, and the couple took a round-the-world tour covered extensively by the press. After Long died in an auto accident in 1906, Mary managed Elitch Gardens alone and went deeply into debt in an attempt to maintain the highest standards. To pay her bills and taxes, in 1916 she sold stock in the park to a group of businessmen led by J. K. Mullen, Mayor Robert Speer, and Ben Stapleton. Mary believed that her friends would eventually return control of the business, but instead they turned over management to John Mulvihill, who subsequently purchased the property. His descendents, the Gurtler family, owned and managed the park for the next eighty-two years.

The new owner continued to make improvements, like the addition of the famous Trocadero Ballroom (despite

Mary's disapproval of public dancing), the Wildcat Roller Coaster, and a Tunnel of Love. Mary lived in her cottage at the park until she died in 1936, surrounded by her beloved animals—mountain sheep, camels, kangaroos, and a white polar bear named Willie. While her pets were alive, she let them wander around her house. When they died, she had them stuffed, like Ed, her famous lion. She turned Willie into a rug.

Elitch Gardens remained Denver's favorite summer amusement for decades, entrancing generations of children and adults with the simplicity of a more graceful era. A high-tech version of the park moved downtown in 1995, becoming part of the Premier Parks Company the following year. At the original park site, the theater and carousel building have been saved to serve as a cultural and community center.

## ❧
# MATING GAMES

Although western women were more independent than their East Coast sisters during the Victorian era, society still considered matrimony the ultimate goal. Young women were steered toward the altar at the first opportunity, provided that the suitor had good character and met the family's expectations. The Victorians had rules for everything, particularly courtship. Among the more affluent, a girl's formal social life began at seventeen, although she was encouraged to wait until twenty-one to marry. Under the watchful eye of a parent or chaperone, she attended dances, concerts, and social events, where she could mingle with the opposite sex. She could also go calling with her mother and receive brief visits from male admirers at home. On New Year's Day, young socialites traditionally accepted gentlemen callers continuously, from early morning until nearly midnight.

Although mutual admiration was supposedly the criterion for a good match, a young woman was expected to marry her social, intellectual, and financial equal or superior. Some experts recommended that the partners be physically very different, so that the children would be less likely to mirror either parent's undesirable features. According to *Hill's Manual of Social and Business Forms*, "the very corpulent should unite with the thin and fair ... the extremely irritable should unite with the lymphatic, the slow and the quiet ... "

"Experts" advised readers to avoid a man who had been particularly successful with women, or a gent with many attentive sisters who might have spoiled him. Above all, she should be wary of a sanctimonious suitor. "Shun a dragon of virtue like a fire," one manual advises. "A man may be good, but he must not overdo it. He who has no wickedness is too good for this world; not even a nun could endure him." Some manuals even addressed matters of sexual compatibility. "Sometimes, even where a woman is endowed with fair physical powers, she consents to marry a man of great amative powers and insatiable sexual nature. The same result is inevitable when a man who is weak and of frail constitution and without powers of endurance marries a woman of strong physical powers and a dominant sexual nature. Such unions often result in alienation, estrangement and sometimes unfaithfulness."

The Victorians were the ultimate romantics, despite all the rules. Couples flirted; spouted poetry; and exchanged flowers, locks of hair, and tokens of love. A young woman was supposed to remain passive in the game, never speaking of her devotion until her suitor proposed marriage. In turn, no gentleman would shower a lady with excessive attention unless he had "honorable intentions." Sentimental love letters were permitted as long as the lovers' parents had editorial control. Rules were relaxed slightly for older couples.

Arranged marriages were still common, particularly among immigrant classes. Once established in America, a family would often look to the "old country" for a suitable bride for their son. In 1914, for example, the author's great-grandparents, the Pagliuso family from southern Italy, arranged marriages for three of their four daughters with families in Las Animas County. (Apparently daughter number four stayed in Italy because she was considered "strange," whatever that meant.) For all practical purposes, the three girls (ages fifteen, sixteen, and seventeen) went directly from the train station to the altar, guarded by chaperones all the way. The bride and groom sometimes met for the first time when exchanging nuptials, which may account for the wary expressions often seen in wedding pictures.

Although immigrant brides had little time to get acquainted with their future spouses, these marriages often worked surprisingly well. *(Guadagnoli wedding photo courtesy of the Rosemary Fetter collection)*

### ❧

# Romancing the Cattle King

*Elizabeth Iliff Warren and John Wesley Iliff*

*T*he sleepy little settlement called Denver got a major economic boost in 1869 with the westward expansion of the railroads. Two years earlier the city's future looked grim when the Union Pacific announced its intention to bypass Denver and build the railroad's main line through Cheyenne, Wyoming. Undaunted, Denverites, led by former governor John Evans and *Rocky Mountain News* editor William Newton Byers, banded together to finance the Denver Pacific Railroad and build a rail spur to Cheyenne. By 1870, a second railroad, called the Kansas Pacific, whistled into Denver, ensuring the city's place as the future rail hub of the Rockies.

The Singer Sewing Machine Company eyed these developments with interest, and in 1869 sent a representative to open a Denver office. Her name was Elizabeth Sarah Fraser, and within a decade she would become the richest woman in Colorado.

"Lizzie" Fraser was born in Fitzroy, Ontario, Canada, on May 24, 1844, the granddaughter of a Scottish army officer who fought in the siege of Quebec during the American Revolution. (Her future husband, J. W. Iliff, joked that his great-grandfather had been hung as a Tory spy during the same war. Although no one believed him, it was true.) Orphaned while still a small child, Lizzie had been raised in Chicago by an aunt, Elizabeth Miller, and her husband, William.

Although Elizabeth had a genteel upbringing, she needed to make her own living. While in her early twenties she found employment with the Singer Sewing Machine Company, at a time when few women were employed outside the home. As an instructor, she would follow up with local agents and teach purchasers of the "newfangled" sewing machines the intricacies of their operation. Impressed by her business acumen, the company sent her to Colorado with another woman to open a branch office in Denver. Although westerners were more supportive of single working women than their East Coast counterparts, this undertaking would prove a challenge for anyone. Lizzie was expected to open new stores, appoint local agents in remote towns, operate the Denver business, and, of course, maintain a pristine reputation.

On July 20, 1868, the *Rocky Mountain News* printed the following announcement:

> We take pleasure in announcing the establishment of an agency of the Singer Sewing Machine Company in Denver by Miss L. S. Fraser of Chicago, assisted by Miss Gray of the same place. They came on Saturday's coach and propose to set an example worthy of their sex by proceeding at once to business and sticking to it. Their goods, 70 to 100 sewing machines, some baby wagons and fancy fixings will be on in about a week. Meanwhile they wish to rent a first class room, ground floor if possible, in neither too public nor too

retired a locality and fit it up in regular Eastern singing—we mean sewing machine style.

The women opened their display room on Larimer Street next door to the *News* office.

Elizabeth met John Wesley Iliff sometime in 1868, an encounter that significantly changed both their lives. As the legend goes, J. W. was driving along a road lined with cabins when he spotted the sprightly young woman making her sales calls. When he offered her a ride in his buggy, Lizzie at first declined and then hesitantly accepted. (According to a less romantic story, John and Lizzie met at the Planter's Hotel in Denver.) Impressed by her "spunk" and good looks, Iliff was instantly smitten. The young cattle king had been widowed since the birth of his son, William, four years earlier.

Like John Wayne, John Wesley Iliff rode tall in the saddle, a true-life western hero. Named after the famous Methodist minister, he grew up on a livestock ranch in the Ohio Valley and attended Ohio Wesleyan University. Restless and ambitious, Iliff left school in 1856. Turning down his father's offer of $7,500 to buy a farm, he instead asked for $500 and headed out West. In April 1857, Iliff opened the first store in a new town called Ohio City, now Princeton, Kansas. After parlaying his original stake into $2,000, he migrated toward Colorado to join the Pikes Peak gold rush. Instead of just a pick and shovel, he and partners Fenton and Auld wisely brought an ox train of groceries and warm clothing to the Cherry Creek settlement.

Thousands of prospectors descended on Denver in 1859, making it easy for J. W. to dispose of his goods at a profit. The skyrocketing price of fresh beef—$40 to $50 a head back East—inspired Iliff and one of his partners to invest in cattle and oxen worn footsore from the long journey to the gold-fields. The entrepreneurs bought these scraggly animals at low prices then wintered the cattle on the dry, short grass near Fort Lupton. By spring, they could be sold for $5^{1}/_{2}$ cents a pound. John kept the prime eastern cattle and some of the Texas long-horns for breeding stock. Soon he owned or controlled more than one hundred miles of grazing land along the Platte River. His reputation for honesty, generosity, and fair dealing helped keep him in business despite Indian raids, grasshopper plagues, and the complete drying of the South Platte in 1863.

Iliff's great career in contracting beef got a jump start in 1866 thanks to Charles Goodnight and Oliver Loving, who forged one of the first big cattle drives from Texas. After the first drive, Iliff bought ten thousand longhorns per year and herded them to his ranch in northeastern Colorado along the now-famous Goodnight-Loving Trail. Iliff's cattle fed the beef-hungry mining camps, Wyoming military forts, and construction crews working on the Union Pacific Railroad. When railroad construction ended, he began shipping dressed carcasses to Chicago in iced railcars. By the time he met Lizzie Fraser, J. W. Iliff had already made a fortune.

When the Singer Sewing Machine Company called Lizzie back to Chicago, Iliff followed, and they were married on March 3, 1870. As a wedding gift, Singer presented them with a treadle sewing machine inlaid with mother-of-pearl. They lived briefly in Cheyenne but moved back to Denver in 1871, partly because of woman's suffrage. Since women could vote in Wyoming, the fastidious Lizzie feared being called for jury duty, since she might be sequestered with gamblers, saloon keepers, and prostitutes. Such squeamishness seems uncharacteristic for a door-to-door saleswoman in the Old West, but of course the dregs of humanity seldom purchased sewing machines. Shortly after the birth of their daughter Edna, John hustled Elizabeth off to Colorado, where women would not vote for another nineteen years.

During the next four years, John and Elizabeth had another daughter, Louise, and a son they named John Wesley Jr. In 1877, John bought the Shaffenberg mansion at 18th and Curtis Streets for his growing family. Despite their happiness, however, Iliff began to experience the effects of a hard life on the range and the consequences of drinking too much alkali water. In December 1877, both he and Lizzie became seriously ill. John had developed serious kidney and gallbladder problems, while Elizabeth, distraught over her husband's illness, had been bedridden following the birth of their son. When noise from traffic passing by their downtown home disturbed the patients, attending physicians stretched ropes across the street at the intersection.

Elizabeth began to improve, but J. W. went downhill. He died surrounded by his family on February 9, 1878, leaving his young widow to raise four children. On the same day, Lizzie received word that cattle thieves were primed to raid the Iliff herds. She gathered her wits and immediately telegraphed their foreman to double the number of ranch hands, which averted the threat.

Amazingly, one of the richest men in Colorado died without a will. As coadministrator of his estate, Lizzie placed experienced cattlemen J. W. Snyder and his brother in charge of the Iliff dynasty. Like her husband, she had a shrewd business sense that enabled her to make a considerable profit and steadily increase the value of the Iliff holdings. Within a few years, the former Singer Sewing Machine saleslady became the wealthiest woman in Colorado.

With the estate under control, Elizabeth Iliff took the children and her "multiple millions" (according to the *Cheyenne Daily Leader*) to visit her Aunt Elizabeth in Chicago. Unfortunately, John Wesley Jr. contracted diphtheria when they returned to Denver and died on April 9, not yet sixteen months old. The loss of her only son so soon after her husband must have been devastating.

Five years after the cattle king's death, Elizabeth Iliff married widower and Methodist minister Bishop Henry White Warren, a clergyman from Massachusetts. Their wedding was the social event of the year, attended by the who's who of Denver. To fill the needs of an expanded family— Warren had two daughters and a stepson from his first marriage—the couple built a large, rust-colored sandstone mansion at 2160 South Cook Street.

In 1884, Mrs. Warren donated $100,000 to the University of Denver to establish the Iliff School of Theology. Although not a particularly religious man, J. W. Iliff had been supportive of a Methodist ministry in Colorado. His widow instructed the university, which was struggling to survive in temporary quarters at 14th and Arapahoe, to raise an additional $50,000 and find a permanent campus before they could receive this bequest. Five years later, the college had raised the necessary funds and moved to University Park in south Denver. Another Iliff mansion on the DU campus, which still stands today, eventually became the headquarters for the Iliff School of Theology.

Elizabeth also outlived Bishop Warren and died on February 14, 1920. Known for her staunch religious convictions and generous contributions to numerous philanthropic causes, she remains one of Colorado's great working-class heroines. She is buried between her two beloved husbands at Fairmount Cemetery.

❧

# THE UPS AND DOWNS OF
# VICTORIAN COIFFEUR

Victorian men considered an ample head of hair very sexy. To create the desired effect, a woman could enhance her crowning glory with hairpieces such as a chignon, curls, braids, or a ponytail that could be knotted in back or on top of the head. Another possibility, the "frizette," consisted of a false front of curls leading from each temple and plaited high in back. Since men found these wigs inconvenient during intimate moments (running their fingers through one could be tricky), women began to grow their own hair down their backs, sometimes all the way to the floor. Of course, men had never bothered with such foolishness themselves since the end of the Revolutionary War, when excess attention to a man's personal appearance smacked of British dandyism and became positively undemocratic.

Although bobby pins weren't invented until the 1920s, several feet of hair could be held in place by wire, pompadour combs, or holders decorated with jewels and flowers. Propriety dictated that only children and prostitutes publicly let their hair down (so to speak), so pioneer women wound their tresses into a simple bun, plait, or topknot. Hairnets, or snoods, kept everything in place.

In 1902, illustrator Charles Dana Gibson popularized the "ultimate look" for the new century. The well-endowed Gibson girl

Denver's stage and screen actress Jobyna Howland became the
original "Gibson girl" after posing for artist Charles Dana Gibson.
*(Courtesy the Denver Public Library, Western History Collection, #H-121)*

sported billowing waves of hair swept up and out over wires or horsehair pads, a style nearly impossible to re-create. To make supporting pads from her own hair, a woman (or more likely her maid) would use strands from her brush. She would comb the hair down in front of her face, place the pads on top of her head, then brush the hair up over the rolls and secure it all with combs. Since finishing spray and mousse were far in the future, she used castor oil, petroleum jelly, or less-benevolent styling aids that contained quicksilver or nitric acid.

In the days before electricity, women curled their hair by lighting a lamp and placing a curling iron on the lamp chimney. A successful procedure resulted in curly ringlets, but the tongs often got too hot and scorched the hair.

To hold large hats in place, ladies used long pins that would reach through the crown of the hat and through the hair, poking out on the other side like unsheathed mini-swords. Since they posed an obvious danger to innocent bystanders, the pins were eventually shortened.

## 🍂
# Gold Dust and Diamonds
*Carrie and Thomas Walsh*

*I*n 1949, Harry Wilson, Inc., purchased the fabulous jewel collection of the late heiress Evalyn Walsh McLean for $1.1 million, roughly $9 million today. The pricey baubles included the rare blue fifty-two-carat Hope Diamond, which probably came from the Kollur Mine in Gloconda, India. According to legend, this particular gem carried a bone-chilling curse. When a jewel thief named Jean Baptiste Tavernier stole the diamond from the neck of a Hindu idol, the angry god arranged a particularly gruesome death for the thief. Still unsatisfied, the vengeful spirit put a curse on the diamond and everyone who would possess it through all eternity. Future owners included Marie Antoinette, the unfortunate queen of France, who was guillotined during the French Revolution.

The diamond's last individual owner, Evalyn Walsh McLean, really did have more than her share of trouble. Despite the incredible fortune she inherited from her father, mining baron Thomas Walsh, she suffered through one emotional crisis after another. In fact, a malicious deity seemed to hover over the entire Walsh family, which was plagued by fatal accidents, suicides, kidnapping threats, and alcohol and drug abuse. Rather than jinxed jewelry, however, Tom Walsh's descendants probably suffered from the curse of overabundance. Although the immigrant Irishman made a place for himself among kings and presidents, Walsh's Midas touch could not protect his dynasty from an unfortunate proclivity toward self-destruction.

An Irish farmer's son, Tom Walsh was born in Tipperary on April 2, 1850. To escape the great famine raging in Ireland, he followed his older brother, Michael, to the United States in 1869. A trained carpenter, he headed west to build bridges for the Colorado Central Railroad. After two years, Tom came down with "gold fever" and drifted through Colorado mining camps until a big strike in the Black Hills lured him to Deadwood. Although modestly successful in South Dakota, he declined a share in the promising Homestake Mine on the advice of other mining men who were old friends. The Homestake later became one of the world's greatest gold producers, keeping the Hearst family in castles and newsprint for the next few generations.

Determined to trust his own instincts in the future, Walsh studied mining until he became an expert. When he returned to Colorado in 1877, he had a $100,000 stake, acquired through his skill as a builder rather than a trader in claims and mines. In Leadville he refurbished an old hotel, which he renamed the Grand. According to journalist Horace Greeley, the Grand attracted a more respectable crowd than the Clarendon, where silver king Horace Tabor later installed his mistress, Baby Doe.

Tom struck it rich romantically when he met the exquisite Carrie Bell Reed. Born in Darlington, Wisconsin, Carrie and her family lived in Birmingham, Alabama, before moving to Denver for her father's health. Her mother, the strong-willed

Anna Reed, was hoping to marry her off to one of Leadville's new millionaires when she insisted that Carrie take a teaching position in the rough mining town. According to Evalyn Walsh McLean in *Father Struck It Rich*, mother and daughter took a bone-jarring stagecoach ride "over a terror-inspiring trail that followed a succession of precipices." Looking out the window, Carrie saw a traffic jam of traders with wagon trains, prospectors on mules and donkeys, and assorted gamblers and shady ladies. Upon their arrival in Leadville, the Reed women immediately established respectability by associating themselves with a local Protestant church.

The Irish Catholic Tom Walsh fell in love at first sound when he accidentally strayed inside the church and heard Carrie sing. Miss Reed reportedly had a soft, musical voice and, according to her daughter, "a figure that men turned to stare at. When she was growing up," said Evalyn, "she had been required to walk around the house for hours balancing a glass of water on her head. Because of these exercises, with her feet—even her toes—concealed underneath a wealth of petticoats, she could, with the utmost elegance, glide so as to appear to be rolling on casters." Tom cut a striking figure himself, standing more than six feet tall with piercing blue eyes and a red handlebar mustache. They married on July 11, 1879.

After managing the Leadville hotel for another year, the couple took off for the mountains to live near the mine Tom had been operating. Their first home, a boxcar set on logs, was not exactly what Anna Reed envisioned for her daughter, but Tom Walsh promised to someday provide his beautiful wife the lavish lifestyle she deserved. On their first anniversary, Carrie's still-besotted husband wrote her the following poem:

*Ah, well I know what priceless luck was mine*
*That brought the day, the hour, when you became my bride.*
*Heaven, indeed, could give no choicer, rarer gift,*
*Than you have been to me, my dear and precious pride,*
*More than life, my darling Carrie Bell.*

After a strike that netted Walsh $75,000, Tom and Carrie briefly moved to Denver. Hard hit by the Depression of 1893, they relocated to Ouray. By this time they had two children, nine-year-old Evalyn and seven-year-old Vinson.

The Walsh family found themselves in a picture-postcard town nestled in a valley, surrounded by 13,000-foot snowcapped peaks and waterfalls cascading down the sheer cliffs. There was little time to enjoy the scenery, for both Tom and Carrie had health problems and money was tight. A hired girl cared for the children so Carrie could travel occasionally to Kansas City and Excelsior Springs, where she sought relief from neuralgia and chronic headaches. As finances dwindled, Walsh continued to prospect the mountains, certain that rich gold deposits could be found around the Imogene Basin, nine miles from Ouray. Occasionally he brought Carrie along, calling her his "good luck charm," although more often Evalyn accompanied him on these expeditions.

Tom originally prospected for low-grade ores such as copper and iron to make a profitable business of his pyrite smelter in Silverton. He soon caught wind of something much

more promising and worked to exhaustion. The doctor recommended complete bed rest, but Tom refused to lie down
for long. When Carrie took a trip Denver to care for her sick
mother, he suffered a relapse. Aching to share his secret, he
called Evalyn into his room one morning. "Remember that
trip we made to the Gertrude?" he asked. "I found gold in
those samples I made that day. Daughter, I've struck it rich!"

In the abandoned silver tunnels of the Camp Bird Mine,
Walsh had discovered a three-foot vein of quartz, which was
gold in tellurium form. He quietly bought up all surrounding
claims and built a smelter and a two-mine tram to bring the
ore from the mine. Remembering his days living in a boxcar,
he built a three-story boardinghouse for the miners with hardwood floors, reading rooms, porcelain bathtubs, hot and cold
running water, and electric lights. With a six-mile gold vein,
Camp Bird became one of the country's largest and most pro-
ductive mines, second only to the Portland in Cripple Creek.
By 1900, properties included 103 mining claims and garnered
between $3 and $4 million a year.

After a train wreck nearly wiped out the entire family,
Tom Walsh decided to embrace the good life while there was
still time. He took the family back East to Washington, D.C.,
where his Irish charm and good looks made him an immedi-
ate social success. With beautiful Carrie at his side, he
entertained presidents McKinley, Roosevelt, and Taft in their
sixty-room mansion at 2020 Massachusetts Avenue, which
included a special suite for the King of Belgium. McKinley
appointed Tom commissioner to the Paris Exposition, and he

later ran for the U.S. Senate, but his egalitarian, humanitarian views were considered dangerous by the rich and powerful. In 1902, against Carrie's wishes, he sold the Camp Bird to a London syndicate for more than $5 million.

The greatest tragedy in Tom and Carrie's life occurred in 1905, when their son, Vinson, who loved fast cars, died in an automobile accident. Evalyn suffered serious injury in the same mishap and required a dangerous operation, which immobilized her for several months and resulted in a morphine addiction. Upon Evalyn's recovery, Tom presented her with a $22,000 Fiat, a strange gift under the circumstances. The Walsh family moved back to Denver in 1906 and purchased the fabulous Wolhurst mansion. Tom pursued his political ambitions, hosting grandiose events for President Taft at Wolhurst. Meanwhile, Evalyn became engaged to Ned McLean, heir to the *Cincinnati Enquirer* and *Washington Post* fortunes. Their $200,000 honeymoon was a round-the-world escapade culminating in the purchase of Evalyn's first exquisite piece of jewelry, a 94.8-carat pear-shaped white diamond called the Star of the East. Her father paid $120,000 for the "combination wedding and Christmas present" when she returned to Denver.

In 1911, Evalyn purchased the Hope Diamond from Pierre Cartier of Paris. At first she disliked the setting, but Cartier made the sale by mounting the jewel as a headpiece on a three-tiered circlet of large white diamonds. He personally brought it to the United States, where he let Evalyn try it out for a weekend. Some time later, the diamond was reset again as a pendant on a diamond necklace.

After Tom Walsh died of lung cancer in 1909, his widow went into a deep depression, refusing to eat or leave her room. Carrie finally came back to life several months later, when Evalyn left her in charge of grandson Vinson while she and Ned went off to France. Carrie became involved in charity work during World War I, turning their Washington, D.C., home into "a clothing factory" that remade old garments for children and widows in France and Belgium. Meanwhile, Evalyn and Ned took their place in society, where Tom's daughter was known for her many acts of generosity and sympathy for the working class. Their Washington, D.C., residence, which Evalyn named "Friendship," became a second home to diplomats and dignitaries, including U.S. presidents Harding and Coolidge. Carrie Walsh died on February 25, 1932, of lung cancer, like her husband.

Evalyn struggled with alcoholism and drug addiction for years. Through an eerie coincidence, her oldest son, Vinson, died in an auto accident like his namesake, at age nine. Ned McLean, also an alcoholic, went insane and had to be confined to an institution. Their two other sons, Jock and Ned, became playboys and alcoholics, while daughter Evalyn died from an overdose of sleeping pills at twenty-five. No direct descendants of the family are alive today.

Many family furnishings, clothing, and other possessions from the Walsh's early days are displayed in the Ouray Museum in southwestern Colorado. The Hope Diamond is now safely ensconced behind a thick glass wall in the Smithsonian Museum of Natural History in Washington, D.C.

## ❧
# **A Military Engagement**
*Mamie Geneva Doud*
*and Dwight David Eisenhower*

One of the Denver's best-known romances escalated into matrimony in a simple brick house at 750 Lafayette Street, where 2nd Lt. Dwight David Eisenhower paid court to nineteen-year-old Marie (Mamie) Geneva Doud. From the days before World War I until the 1960s, the prestigious couple often spent holidays and vacations in the large foursquare that later became known as "the Denver White House."

The second of four daughters, Mamie was born to John and Elvira Doud on November 14, 1896. John Doud made a fortune in the meatpacking business and opted for semiretirement in 1905, moving the family from Iowa to Colorado, first Pueblo and later Colorado Springs. Mamie's sister Eleanor had a heart condition affected by higher altitudes, so the family finally settled in Denver. A doting father, Doud provided the girls with a comfortable lifestyle, sending Mamie to Corona School and Miss Wolcott's Finishing School for young ladies.

During a winter vacation in San Antonio, Texas, the pretty socialite met 2nd Lt. Dwight D. Eisenhower, who later described her as "a vivacious and attractive girl, smaller than average, saucy in the look about her face and her whole attitude."

The encounter would change her life.

Dwight David Eisenhower was a self-made man, the third of five sons born to a farmer in Abilene, Kansas. After Eisenhower graduated from high school, he worked in a creamery, partly to enable one of his older brothers to attend college. Since money was scarce for his own education, he took the competitive examinations for both the U.S. Naval Academy at Annapolis and the U.S. Military Academy at West Point. Eisenhower wanted to serve in the Navy, but at twenty-one the military considered him too old for Annapolis, so he settled for West Point.

Ike courted Mamie with the same determination that he later directed at the German Army, and the couple announced their engagement on Valentine's Day 1916. Although Mamie admitted that she had been spoiled and pampered, she gritted her teeth and promised to become the best of military wives. They married in her parents' Denver home at noon on July 1, 1916, in a ceremony attended only by the family. After a brief Colorado honeymoon, they returned to Fort Sam Houston, where Eisenhower was attached to the 19th Infantry. While Ike was overseas, Mamie often returned to Denver, resuming her role as social belle and trendsetter. She was once asked to leave the floor during a formal tea dance at Elitch's Trocadero Ballroom because she was dancing cheek to cheek—with her uncle!

During the military years, Mamie followed Eisenhower around the world, moving thirty-seven times in twenty-seven years. The couple had two sons, one of whom died in infancy. In 1936, the Douds deeded their house to Mamie, who often returned to her parents' home when she was unable to join her husband. The most critical separation came during World War II, when Ike and Mamie were apart three years while he commanded U.S. forces in Europe.

In Germany, Eisenhower allegedly began an affair with his secretary and driver, a former British model named Kay Sommersby Morgan. In 1976, after Ike had been dead for seven years, the lady wrote a "tell-all" book called *Past Forgetting* in order to pay her medical bills. Former president Harry Truman later substantiated her story, maintaining that Ike had written to General Marshall asking permission to divorce Mamie and marry Kay. When the Pentagon denied the request, Eisenhower opted to save his career. Before leaving office, Truman purportedly destroyed all correspondence. True or not, the marriage survived.

After Eisenhower became president, the couple made Denver their vacation retreat, residing alternately at Mamie's parents' home, the Brown Palace Hotel, and Lowry Air Force Base. Ike golfed at Cherry Hills Country Club and went fishing at the Byers Park Ranch, owned by his good friend Askel Neilson. On one occasion, Vice President Richard Nixon supposedly entertained the family by playing the piano in the basement of the Lafayette Street house.

Eisenhower suffered a heart attack in Denver on September 24, 1955. When he emerged from Fitzsimmons Hospital the following month, he posed for photographs in bright red pajamas embroidered at Denver's Daniels & Fisher store that said "Much Better, Thanks." Ike made a full recovery and won reelection to a second term. The couple retired to a farm in Gettysburg, Pennsylvania, where Ike died in 1969 and Mamie followed ten years later. They are buried near a small chapel on the grounds of the Eisenhower Library in Abilene, Kansas.

## 🐦

# **A Simple Strand of Pearls**
*Agnes and Harry Heye Tammen*

*H*arry Heye Tammen fell in love with Agnes Reid the moment he saw her … almost. According to the great storyteller Gene Fowler, they met when Harry caught her stealing wood from his lumber pile and chased her nearly a block, which was a lot of exercise for the nonathletic Tammen. Agnes later explained that she had taken the boards on a dare, but by then it didn't matter. She had the kind of gumption that the future cofounder of the *Denver Post* admired.

A sprightly sixteen-year-old with dark hair and a sparkle in her eye, Agnes had recently moved to Denver from Petersburg, Virginia, with her parents. At the time, Harry was a recent widower who operated a curio shop at the Windsor Hotel. To impress Agnes, he took her to see his feature attraction, Moon-Eye, the petrified Indian maiden, in truth the remains of a well-preserved senior citizen that Tammen had purchased from a bankrupt embalmer. Moon-Eye made Agnes slightly nauseous, but she liked Harry a lot. They were married two years later, and the romance lasted a lifetime.

Tammen was a combination con artist, entertainer, and crusader, a cheerful man who never lost his childlike zest for life. Born in Baltimore on March 6, 1856, Harry had been named for his father, Heye Heinrich Tammen, a minor official with the Netherlands Consulate. When the senior Tammen died unexpectedly, seventeen-year-old Harry quit school and set out on his own. His mother's parting words were "Go with love and good cheer." When he became a success, Harry always signed his letters, "Yours with love and good cheer."

Nicknamed "The Little Dutchman" because he stood only five feet three inches, the plump entrepreneur became proprietor of a Baltimore saloon by the time he was twenty, and then moved on to Chicago. Around 1880 he drifted into Denver, alternately working at the Windsor Hotel as a bell-hop, busboy, bouncer, and bartender. After marrying his Baltimore sweetheart, Elizabeth Evans, Harry opened up a curio shop, selling everything from mineral specimens to "authenticated scalps" and fake Navajo blankets. His first journalistic endeavor was a promotional newsletter for his business, called *The Great Divide*.

Harry's first wife died in 1890, just after he finished building her a beautiful new home. Two years later he married Agnes Reid, who was twenty years his junior. The exact opposite of Harry, who always loved center stage, Agnes remained in the background and concentrated on charity work. Although both of her parents were Scottish immigrants, she never fit the tightfisted stereotype. Mrs. Tammen later explained her generosity with the quip, "There are two kinds of Scots. I'm the other kind." An intelligent, well-informed

Harry Tammen loved celebrity while his wife, Agnes, quietly devoted her life to charity work. *(Courtesy of the Denver Public Library, Western History Collection, #F-4682 and #F-23527)*

conversationalist and a good listener, she had a quick wit and a sharp sense of humor. She needed it, because life with Harry had to be a real adventure.

Harry met future *Denver Post* cofounder Fred Bonfils in Chicago, sometime around 1895. Tammen was trying to sell tinted photographs of the 1893 World's Fair, but he was also looking for a backer for his latest scheme—the purchase of Denver's faltering *Evening Post.* Tammen had been hit hard by the recent depression and was practically broke at the time. When he saw some lottery tickets printed by a gambler named Fred Bonfils, he resolved to meet the gentleman. For some reason, the perpetually suspicious Bonfils trusted Tammen and agreed to finance purchase of the eight-page daily newspaper, which they renamed *The Denver Evening Post.* While

Bonfils supplied the business sense, bombastic energy, and start-up cash, Harry's assets included vision, imagination, and a wonderful sense of humor. Both had plenty of bravado and charisma. As a team, they were unbeatable.

Over the years, the showman in Harry led the *Post* into bizarre enterprises, such as purchase of the Sells-Floto Circus (he loved elephants), and weird campaigns, such as the attempt to free convicted Colorado cannibal Alfred Packer. Harry purposefully created an image of himself as a con man (like P. T. Barnum) and a rube, but actually he was a generous man who built a fortune, then gave much of it away.

Although Fred Bonfils had no sense of humor, Harry liked to play jokes on readers, which he did just often enough to keep them awake. The Little Dutchman carried off one of his most successful pranks in 1908, just after the city completed an expensive new auditorium to house the Democratic National Convention. A few days before the convention, a shocking banner headline announced that the beautiful new structure had perished in a blazing inferno. A photo of firemen pouring water on a burning building accompanied an eight-column story. Those who had the patience to wade through a detailed description of the tragedy found the final sentence printed in small type: "After a thorough investigation, the *Post* has discovered that every word of the story is untrue." Surprisingly, Denverites thought this was hilarious.

Unlike other newspaper moguls (such as his partner Bonfils and *Rocky Mountain News* founder William Byers),

Tammen remained true to his wife throughout their marriage. Both Harry and Agnes loved children, although they never had any of their own. Harry's favorite story about Agnes concerned a string of pearls that built a new wing of Children's Hospital.

Among the couple's many friends was J. Ogden Armour, heir to the Chicago grain and meatpacking fortune. When Agnes expressed admiration for a pearl necklace worn by Mrs. Armour at a party, Harry determined to buy his wife an equally impressive trinket. Shortly before Christmas 1921, Harry handed Agnes a $100,000 check "for the string of pearls you wanted." With mixed emotions, Agnes replied that it was a shame to spend so much money on a necklace when her pet project, the Children's Hospital, was badly in need of a new wing. She asked Harry to give the money to the hospital instead. The Agnes Reid Tammen Memorial wing eventually cost nearly $200,000, and Harry later gave Agnes a less expensive pearl necklace.

By the time the hospital wing opened in February 1924, Tammen knew his time was running short. He died of cancer on July 19 at age sixty-eight, leaving 20 percent of his *Denver Post* stock to Children's Hospital. Assuming stewardship of the Tammen fortune, Agnes took a trip through Europe and the Far East in 1927, seeking out clinics and medical facilities that specialized in the care of children. After she returned to Denver, an automobile accident left her bedridden for several months. Upon recovery, she began work on Harry Tammen Hall, a training school and home for nurses.

Thanks to Mrs. Tammen, the hospital later added a $200,000 hydrotherapy wing for treatment of children with polio. After visiting a New Zealand hospital in 1936, she changed the colored tiles in the hydrotherapy pool to blue, so that children would be aware that water reflects the sky. Her warmth and personal touches helped to make Children's one of the best-equipped hospitals of its kind in the country. When told that she spent too much money on charitable causes and should be more conservative for her own sake, she retorted, "None of this I can take with me. This is not mine, but something left to me in trust."

The entire city mourned Agnes Tammen's death in July 1942. In a front-page newspaper story, reporter Frances Wayne wrote, "Her profound love for humanity raised philanthropy among the fine arts." The Tammen Trust still contributes to the support of Children's Hospital.

ও

# LOVE TOKENS
# AND TALISMANS

The Victorians attached special meanings to all things romantic,
including gifts exchanged between lovers. Gloves and gauntlets
were always popular, since they signified honesty and friendly
intentions. A gentleman might give his lady a fan to spark the
flame of love, while a pair of doves bespoke marital harmony.
Another romantic gift, the silver spoon, stood for purity and true
beauty, particularly when decorated with a scallop shell symbolic
of the love goddess Aphrodite.

Love jewelry spoke its own language. A locket decorated
with a romantic emblem or an inscription represented love
locked deep within the heart, particularly if it contained a
photograph or a lock of hair. A gold chain and anchor meant
constancy, while love knots and rings symbolized passion without
end. Love jewelry could even be suggestive, such as a bracelet
shaped to look like a corset with laces and buttons. A lady knew
that she had captured her lover's heart if she received a link
bracelet with a tiny lock and key.

Victorian men often expressed romantic sentiments
through "regard" or message jewelry. A ring or brooch might be
set with six gemstones, ruby, emerald, garnet, amethyst, another
ruby (or perhaps a rhodochrosite for Coloradans), and diamond.

The first letter of each stone would spell out the word "regard." Another popular combination, lapis, opal, vermeil (a type of garnet), and emerald, spelled out "love." Each gem had a special meaning. Pearls were a symbol of tears, while rubies signified passion, and emeralds meant fidelity. Coral warded off illness and evil, while garnets empowered the wearer, and sapphires ensured fidelity.

According to the rules of propriety, Victorian courting couples kept their distance. *(Courtesy of the Rosemary Fetter collection with special thanks to Bill Bower)*

# The Good Life

*Julie and Spencer Penrose*

Julie and Spencer Penrose were born to be rich. With panache seldom seen in modern-day jet setters, the gregarious couple reveled in a lifestyle that most people can only imagine. For nearly three decades they trekked about the globe, sailing aboard luxury liners and collecting art treasures for their Colorado Springs villa and the elegant Broadmoor Hotel. They purchased a cozy cottage in Hawaii and a spacious Parisian apartment, stayed at the best hotels in Europe and the Orient, tasted the finest cuisine, wore the most stylish clothing, and drank the best liquor. Most important, unlike many of their class, Julie and Spencer Penrose had a rollicking good time.

A blue blood with a taste for high living, Spencer (aka Speck) Penrose could trace his lineage back to Bartholomew Penrose, partner to Pennsylvania founder William Penn. The fourth of six sons born to Dr. R. A. F. and Sarah Penrose, Spencer grew up in a wealthy family of overachievers. Generations of prominent Penrose Philadelphians included Speck's father, the city's leading obstetrician and gynecologist and founder of Children's Hospital. An admirer of the Spartan lifestyle, Dr. Penrose strongly advocated exercise, temperance, and a healthy diet. Most of his children totally ignored his advice once they were out of the house.

Spencer's parents were both deeply involved in their sons' education, and the boys were expected to excel academically. Although intelligent and handsome in a chilly sort of way, Spencer had trouble keeping up with the precocious clan. His older brothers, Charles, Boies, and Dick, won top scholastic honors at Harvard, but Speck had been lucky to graduate. While his athletically accomplished brother Dick spurred Harvard's rowing team to victory for two years straight, Speck tried out for the same crew and permanently injured the retina of his eye. And, no matter how much he drank and raised hell, Speck had older brothers who were better at that, too, according to the president of Harvard.

Penrose apparently bore no grudges, but to avoid any more unfavorable comparisons with siblings, he headed West at the first opportunity. To gain his father's approval and shed the black sheep image, Speck aimed to get very rich very quickly. After four uneventful years in New Mexico, he joined a former pal from Philadelphia named Charles Tutt in Colorado Springs, making his debut in a brawl at the Cheyenne Mountain Country Club. For the next three years, Penrose dabbled in local real estate, wheeling and dealing by day and partying every night. He reportedly became involved with a pretty horse trainer named Sarah Elizabeth Halthusen but ended the affair after his older brothers made a special trip to Cripple Creek to talk him out of it.

Penrose and Tutt sold the C. O. D. Mine for $250,000, then built a successful refinery in Colorado City. In 1903, a mill employee named Daniel Jackling convinced them to invest in a scheme to process low-grade copper ore in Bingham Canyon, Utah. The Utah Copper Company made a fortune, and in 1909 the Penrose problem child raked in more than a million a year after taxes. Richer than his father and brothers combined, Speck joined the rest of the family on a list of *Who's Who in America*. No great friend of the working class, he once said that a man in overalls wasn't worth more than $3 a day.

An eminently eligible bachelor, Penrose had been instructed by his father and unmarried brothers to escape entanglements that might lead to matrimony. At age thirty-nine he finally met his match in Julie Villers Lewis MacMillan. An attractive widow in her early thirties, Julie had also grown up in a large and wealthy family of blue bloods, albeit much less austere than the Penrose clan. From her French forebearers, Julie had inherited a lively disposition and a taste for the good life. While still a teenager and the belle of Detroit society (her father was the mayor), she married the boy next door, James Howard MacMillan. Considered a great catch, the groom was the son of U.S. Senator James MacMillan, a millionaire statesman who had become one of the nation's largest manufacturers of railroad cars.

Like many young aristocrats inspired by the dashing Teddy Roosevelt, Julie's husband enlisted in the Spanish-American War and shipped off to Cuba. He returned home in poor health after a bout with malaria that resulted in pulmonary tuberculosis. In 1900, the couple moved to Colorado Springs, hoping that Jim would regain his health. He lost the battle in May 1902, just three weeks after their only son had died of appendicitis. Following a lengthy period of mourning, Julie tossed aside the black veil and rejoined the Colorado Springs social set. When she set her pretty blue eyes on Spencer Penrose at a Cheyenne Mountain Country Club clambake, the recalcitrant bachelor was doomed.

Julie pursued Speck sweetly and relentlessly, feeding his taste for fine cuisine along with his ego and sending her staff to do his laundry. No one suspected the young widow of being a gold digger, since she had a considerable inheritance of her own. After two years Spencer realized that he had become dependent upon her, panicked, and joined brother Dick on a European cruise. Julie outsmarted him and booked passage on the same cruise, supposedly en route to Europe to enroll her daughter Gladys in a private school at Brussels. His resolve slipping away, Penrose offered to drive Julie and her friend Edith through the south of France in his touring car.

Spencer finally accepted the inevitable and asked his brother to seek their father's approval of the match. Dick wrote the senior Penrose

> Speck seems very much devoted to her and she equally so to him … He can't read much on account of his eye and … is not interested in any particular subject that would lead him to seek amusement from

Julie Penrose thought she should be treated like a queen, and her husband, Spencer, willingly obliged. *(Courtesy of the Tom Noel collection)*

literary or scientific sources. He is, therefore, peculiarly dependent on social intercourse. As he himself said to me the other day, he "cannot sit down at eight o'clock in the evening and read until bed time," nor can he go on forever drinking rum at clubs. Therefore he seems to think his only refuge is to get married. …

With his father's blessings, Spencer proposed to Julie by dropping a note into her lap while she was sunbathing on a beach in the French Riviera. They married on April 26, 1906, and honeymooned in Spain and France. "Speck and his wife are here [in France] and seem to be very happy," Dick reported to Dr.

Penrose. "They are starting today on a several weeks trip to Tours and Vichy, in France, in their automobile. They asked me to go with them, but I thought that perhaps people on a honeymoon were more happy alone." This turned out to be a wise decision on Dick's part, since the car fell apart during the journey.

Despite Speck's initial reticence, the couple had a wonderful marriage. Julie's warmth and kindness provided a mellowing influence on her still-insecure husband. In return she expected to be treated like a queen, and Spencer did his best. Not surprisingly, their lifestyle became more flamboyant two years after their marriage, following the death of Speck's father. After Julie's daughter Gladys married Belgian Count Cornet de Ways Ruart in 1914, they made frequent visits to Europe. No matter how much money they spent, they just got richer.

The Penroses entertained lavishly in their fabulous Mediterranean villa called El Pomar Estate in Colorado Springs. Famous for the showiest affairs in town, they held rambunctious parties and banquets that reflected the spirit of the Roaring Twenties. Spencer had always been a hard drinker, and the bar was always stocked with liquor, even during Prohibition. "I think you and Julie are having some fun out of life, more than anybody I know," *Denver Post* publisher Fred Bonfils once told Spencer. "I am glad you both have sense enough to enjoy it as you go along."

The creation of the Broadmoor Hotel in 1918 became one of the greatest Penrose accomplishments. Legend has it that Speck built his own hotel partly to spite the management of the Colorado Springs Antlers Hotel, which refused to allow him to ride a horse into the bar. The elegant Broadmoor soon became a playground for the wealthy international set, a reflection of Spencer's marketing ability and Julie's good taste. Positively awash in European décor and fine art, the Broadmoor featured hand-painted frescoes and ceilings of the sort generally found in Italian cathedrals. A doting Spencer had Julie's personal trademark, the swan, painted near the elevator and above the fireplace in the center terrace. Several of the beautiful, temperamental birds were relocated from Canada to Broadmoor Lake.

The Penrose fondness for animals was evident in their personal menagerie, which included an elephant named Tessie, supposedly a gift from the Rajah of Nagpur. When one guest sued after being bitten by a monkey, Spencer moved the primates, coyotes, snakes, bears, and giraffes to the Cheyenne Mountain Zoo, which he created in 1926. Julie generally restricted her pets to small dogs with names like Pitty Pat.

Mrs. Penrose enjoyed playing the role of Lady Bountiful and Spencer cheerfully supported her numerous charities, particularly those associated with the arts. Over the years she contributed generously to the Colorado Springs Fine Arts Center and helped fund the revival of the Central City Opera House in the 1930s. Two years before his death in 1939, Spencer set up the El Pomar Association, bequeathing his $40 million estate as its base. One of Colorado's most affluent foundations, El Pomar has made substantial contributions to several charities and activities, including the Colorado Springs Symphony and the Boys Club of America.

Julie outlived Spencer by nearly two decades. A beautiful woman well into her sunset years, she filled her days with charity work, threw dinner parties, entertained foreign dignitaries, and enjoyed her great-grandchildren. She still loved ocean cruises and planned another trip abroad in 1955, when her doctor discovered cancer after a routine checkup. The Queen of the Broadmoor died on January 23, 1956, at age eighty-five, surrounded by several close friends and family members.

### CHAPTER V

# Rugged Individualists

❧

## A Red Rose for Madge

*Madge Smiley Reynolds and
Fredrick Gilmer Bonfils*

Only the perverse nature of sexual attraction can explain the rapport between Fred Bonfils, the vitriolic founder of the *Denver Post*, and Madge Reynolds, the saint of Denver society. No two people could have been less alike. A con artist and creative genius, Bonfils had been blessed with the handsome, chiseled profile of an actor (which he once was), the zeal of a dedicated reformer (which he never really was), and the business acumen of a loan shark. Madge Smiley Reynolds, on the other hand, spread sunshine wherever she went. A lady beloved throughout the city for her charity and compassion, she was a poet, crusader, and the sister of noted historian Jerome Smiley. While Fred was known for his stranglehold on the almighty dollar, Madge lived simply despite her wealth and station, taking orphans into her home and defending the downtrodden like a local Joan of Arc. Interestingly, their affair remained remarkably circumspect despite the fact that Fred had a wife.

A wheeler-dealer of Corsican descent, Fredrick Gilmer Bonfils came from an upper-middle class family in Troy, Missouri. Admitted to West Point at seventeen, he left the academy before graduating, unfairly attributing his dismissal to a decision to marry Belle Barton from New York. (He actually failed math, an odd beginning for the future business genius of the *Denver Post*.) During Bonfils's colorful career, Belle remained in the background, visible mainly at charity events, Christmas parties, and Sunday services. Although Fred saw himself as a dedicated family man, he controlled his wife and children like a domestic Napoleon, particularly his daughters May and Helen. While May rebelled outright by marrying the family chauffeur, Helen stayed in his good graces long enough to acquire control of the newspaper after he and partner, Harry Tammen, were gone.

Bonfils and Tammen purchased the faltering *Evening Post* in 1895, adding the word "Denver" and changing the face of local journalism forever. While they had little experience in newspaper publishing, the bombastic duo knew instinctively what would grasp the public's always-wavering attention. The *Post* successfully positioned itself as the champion of the people, often reading like a combination of *True Crime* and *True Confession* magazine. (One of Fred's brainstorms, a series of interviews with obstetricians, was slapped with the banner headline "Does It Hurt to Be Born?") Although the *Post*

Despite his marriage and family, dynamic *Denver Post* co-founder Fredrick Gilmer Bonfils fell for poet and social crusader Madge Reynolds. *(Courtesy of the Denver Public Library, Western History Collection, #F-19958)*

supplied the city with plenty of melodrama and comic relief, the paper also provided a real public service, fighting political and social injustices in a system rampant with abuse.

Madge Reynolds first approached Fred Bonfils in February 1903 on a typical errand of mercy. The widow of a

Continental Oil executive, Madge was in her early thirties at the time, a soft-spoken honey blonde with violet eyes and a sweet disposition. Mrs. Reynolds hoped to elicit the *Post's* support in a campaign to release a young man from prison. Antone Woode had been sentenced at age ten to life imprisonment for murder. By age twenty, his intelligence and cooperative attitude made him a great candidate for parole. Madge had been on the verge of obtaining his release when he participated in a prison break, an unwise decision that put him back to square one with the authorities after his capture.

Enchanted by Woode's benefactress, Bonfils immediately took up the young man's cause. The publisher had never been subject to twittering of the heart, but his first editorial said more about his feeling for Madge than the situation of the prisoner:

> Fortunate, indeed, is Antone Woode to have so eloquent, untiring and forceful a champion to plead in his behalf. Refined, educated, earnest with a wide circle of influential friends and a liberal supply of money to help the cause along, nobody is in a position to do so much for the boy murderer as is Mrs. Reynolds. Her plea is plaintive, her argument amazing, her eloquence effective and her perseverance pervading. With such an attorney, the chains of Prometheus might have been stricken off.

This was heady stuff, even in an age of flowery rhetoric.

Although her closest friends included Bonfils's worst enemies, especially *Rocky Mountain News* publisher Thomas
Patterson, Fred considered Madge a goddess and began calling her "dearest." They met frequently in Bonfils's office and
soon began taking long horseback rides together. Although
Madge often invited male guests to her home, which had
become an informal salon for the city's intelligentsia, she seldom saw any man individually. Fortunately, her reputation
precluded any gossip, even when she began entertaining Fred
alone. According to Gene Fowler in *Timberline,* they would
relax in her cozy kitchen to sample half-pint bottles of champagne and eat the cake she baked herself, since she had no
servants. If they did anything else, no one talked about it.

Their relationship continued for nearly two years, with
a temporary cooling of affections after a violent episode
involving the *Post*'s two-fisted editor and Madge's friend
Thomas Patterson. When the *News* printed an editorial that
labeled Fred a criminal and blackmailer who should be in
prison, Bonfils retaliated by punching Patterson in the face
and breaking his palate. After a lengthy editorial war and a
public trial, the court fined Bonfils $50 and warned him to
limit further attacks to newsprint. Madge forgave Fred when
he promised to behave like a gentleman in the future.

One of the worst tragedies of Fred Bonfils's life occurred
on February 22, 1908, when Mrs. Reynolds died suddenly
and unexpectedly. Although Madge's health had never been in
question, doctors attributed her passing to angina. Fred
mourned the loss with a ferocity that frightened his friends.

The couple had gone horseback riding together on the day before she died, and Madge reportedly had returned home in a highly emotional state. Some gossips concluded that Fred had ended the relationship, and Madge really died of a broken heart or committed suicide. Others, judging from the publisher's hysterical reaction to his lady's demise, thought he had proposed marriage instead and they were about to begin a new life together. Bonfils never commented one way or the other, and nobody had the courage to ask.

Denver newspapers printed daily accolades to Madge's virtues and the *Post* even published some of her poetry, excerpted below:

### Cliff Palace

> *I've dreamed that when the midnight moon*
> *The half-world floods below,*
> *Its hoary phantoms burst their bonds*
> *And wander to and fro,*
> *Till with the dawn's soft-stealing light*
> *Reluctantly they glide*
> *Back to the mighty sepulcher*
> *Where all their kindred bide*

On the day of Madge's funeral, Bonfils stood apart from the services, watching from the back of the crowd. Her pallbearers included his worst enemies—Patterson, Denver Tramway magnate William Gray Evans, and corporate attorney Thomas J. O'Donnell. According to Fowler, Fred stepped forward through the crowd as they lowered her casket into the ground. He plucked a single flower from a blanket of red roses, placed it gently on her casket, and walked away.

Bonfils often spoke of Mrs. Reynolds, although not without a touch of sadness. He kept her letters at hand so that he could always refer to them. No matter which one he read, he always found an important message from Madge, who remained his "dearest" until he died in 1933.

*Note: Although the publication founded by Bonfils and Tammen bears little similarity to today's* Denver Post, *the paper's editorial page still carries Bonfils's original cryptic slogan: "There is no hope for the satisfied man."*

### ❧
# **Against All Odds**
### *Madam C. J. Walker*

On July 20, 1905, Sarah Breedlove stepped off the train at Union Station, an attractive dark-skinned woman of thirty-eight who was on her way to becoming a millionaire. In her valise, Sarah carried a supply of Pope-Turnbo Wonderful Hair Grower, a concoction that would find a receptive market among the city's African American female population.

Working as a boardinghouse cook for $30 a month, Sarah began selling the hair product as a sideline. During spare moments, she mixed tubs of hair restorer with ingredients obtained from the local drugstore, testing and experimenting with each batch. Eventually she quit the kitchen and rented an attic on Clarkson Street, where she developed her own formula. After a time she broke with her former employer, Annie Pope-Turnbo, and began marketing the product as Madam Walker's Wonderful Hair Grower.

Sarah had charisma and confidence in the benefits of her work, which lent credibility to her sales pitch. Hair loss and breakage was a serious problem for African American women, particularly in Denver where the soil was alkaline and the humidity low. Madam Walker's sulfur-based formula could alleviate the condition when combined with a regimen of frequent washing, scalp massage, and improved nutrition. Since the city's relatively small African American population of 4,000 clustered within a few blocks of the Five Points area, the product could easily be sold door to door. As word filtered through the community, her client list grew.

At first glance, Sarah Breedlove seems an unlikely candidate for great commercial achievement. Born in 1867, she was the fifth child of former slaves who had become sharecroppers on their former master's Louisiana estate. After losing her parents by age seven, she moved to Vicksburg to live with her sister and brother-in-law, whom she later described as cruel and abusive. "I married at the age of fourteen in order to get a home of my own," she later explained to a reporter.

Sarah's rarely spoke of her first husband, Moses McWilliams, who died in 1888 leaving her with a three-year-old daughter, Lelia. He may have been lynched during a race riot, a tragic but common occurrence in the postbellum South. Sarah headed north to be near family in Saint Louis and found work as a laundress. Six years later, she married John Davis, a miscreant who drank excessively, kept another woman on the side, and physically abused her. Yearning for a better life for her daughter, Sarah saved enough money to send the girl to Knoxville College and enrolled in night school. Without a backward glance she left John Davis in 1902 and began seeing Charles Joseph (C. J.) Walker, a good-looking mulatto who worked as a reporter and sold subscriptions and advertising. Unfortunately, she never got around to divorcing Davis, who later claimed part of her estate.

C. J. joined Sarah in Denver and they were married in January 1906. A gregarious showman who promoted Sarah's enterprise while running his own business, Walker opened up the Industrial Real Estate and Loan Company at 212 15th Street. Sharpening her marketing skills, Sarah bought ads in Denver's African American newspaper, the *Colorado Statesman*, and began calling herself Madam C. J. Walker. She traveled along the Front Range to Boulder, Colorado Springs, Pueblo, and Trinidad, conducting classes in scalp massage and selling her formula. In September 1906, the Walkers moved on to the southern and eastern states "to place their product on the market and start a mail order business."

In 1912, Sarah divorced C. J. after discovering that (1) he had squandered and mismanaged her money, and (2) he was having an affair with her representative Dora Larrie. Walker would spend the next few years unsuccessfully attempting to get back in her good graces.

The Madam C. J. Walker Manufacturing Company expanded to include additional hair care products, cosmetics, cleansing cream, cold cream, and face powder. Sarah developed innovative distribution strategies for her products that allowed thousands of African American women an economic freedom that they would never have achieved otherwise. She also became a political activist and philanthropist whose substantial contributions helped restructure the YWCA and NAACP.

On May 25, 1919, the most prominent and wealthiest black woman in the country died of nephritis at fifty-two, leaving her daughter, Lelia, to run the business. Sarah Breedlove Walker, a former cook and laundress, left a $600,000 estate, worth more than $6 million in today's currency.

## ❧

# The Black Widow of Humboldt Street
*Lena Allen Webster-Stoiber-Rood-Ellis*
*and Husbands*

When Lena Stoiber died in Stresa, Italy, in 1935, nobody cared very much except her hairdresser, who enjoyed an unexpected $10,000 windfall. Twenty years earlier Lena had been one of Denver's wealthiest society women, an eccentric who built "spite walls" to annoy her neighbors and threw temper tantrums when she didn't get her own way. Imperious, sharp-tongued, and high living, she dealt out misery to anyone who dared ruffle her elegant feathers. She also married four times, something of a record in the days when men usually outlived their wives. Interestingly, three of her husbands died or disappeared under strange circumstances.

Lena Allen-Webster-Stoiber-Rood-Ellis first appeared in Grand Junction around 1882, the wife of a lawyer named F. C. Webster. She had changed her name from "Helen" because she thought that it lacked dramatic impact. Lena made an instant impression on folks because of her good looks, buxom figure, and notoriously nasty temper. On one occasion she gave the town's young postmaster a tongue lashing because her mail went astray, an experience so traumatic that he wrote a scathing newspaper article about her fifty years later.

In 1884, Lena and her husband packed up and moved to Silverton, where Mr. Webster opened a law office. Reports vary as to whether Webster died mysteriously or disappeared mysteriously, but a few months later Lena announced her engagement to German mining engineer and metallurgist Edward Stoiber. A brilliant mining expert, Stoiber was among the first to treat low-grade ores at a profit, making a fortune on the Silver Lake Mine. He built a beautiful home for Lena, which they called Waldheim.

During the Silverton days, Lena had a few good deeds to her credit. "The Bonanza Queen" treated the miners well, running a boardinghouse and sponsoring dances or other entertainment for the workers. At Christmas she liked to play Santa, delivering toys to Silverton's children on a sleigh. During the Depression of 1893, she helped Stoiber keep the mine going by sheer determination, overseeing the workers alone when necessary. Nicknamed "Captain Jack" for her horsemanship and colorful language, she was also an early preservationist whose efforts helped establish Mesa Verde as a national park.

Unfortunately, Lena received the most publicity by building "spite fences," a bad habit she eventually brought with her to Denver. After a quarrel with a Silverton neighbor named Hand, she purchased the adjoining lot and built an ugly barn to annoy him. When Hand's friends later bought their house, she put up a high fence to obstruct the view. After the occupants added another story to their house, Lena topped the fence with billboards.

After Edward Stoiber sold out his mining interests to Guggenheim, the couple moved to Denver and bought lots for a new home at 10th and Humboldt. Stoiber drew up a plan for "Stoiberhof," a three-story French Renaissance estate of light brick with white stone trimming. In their typical neighborly fashion, the Stoibers planned to surround the home with a stone wall.

Edward and Lena took off for Europe in 1903, leaving the house plans in the hands of the architects. The following April, Denver friends received word that Edward Stoiber had died in Paris following the onset of a sudden illness, reportedly typhoid. Lena shipped him back to Denver and installed his remains in an expensive Fairmount Cemetery mausoleum, then proceeded with plans for the house. In 1919, her third husband, Seattle lumber baron Hugh Rood joined her at Stoiberhof. Although the couple appeared to be very happy, Lena still dedicated every April 21 to Edward Stoiber on the anniversary of his death.

The Stoiber and Rood millions gained Lena instant acceptance as a member of Denver's Sacred 36, the moniker for a group that often met for nine tables of cards at the estate of society queen Louise Hill. Lena's fiery temper and unpredictability made people uncomfortable, and soon she received few invitations, while hers were being declined. Before long she was quarreling with another neighbor, Egbert W. Reed. Lena retaliated as usual, this time putting up a twelve-foot-high brick wall. After some research, Reed discovered that the wall encroached an inch onto his property, and he got a court order to move the fence. As the case dragged through the courts for months, Lena angrily stomped off to Europe, telling Reed in no uncertain terms exactly what he could do with the wall. He eventually accepted a $1 settlement and moved to California.

April was apparently a bad month for Lena's husbands. On the night of April 14, 1912, the ocean liner *Titanic* struck an iceberg on its maiden voyage. When the big ship went down, Rood was among the 1,500 supposed dead. Lena might have gone down with him except for a last-minute decision to remain in London for another week. As she raced to Halifax after the disaster, she continued to hear rumors that her husband had survived. Although tales of passengers picked up by small vessels were common, few were as persistent as the stories about Rood. New York and Denver police, and even Scotland Yard, were for a time besieged with reports that he had been seen in some location or other. Lena spent a fortune on private investigators, but no trace of her husband emerged. Years later the *Denver Post* received a letter from someone who might have been Rood, asking if Lena was still alive.

The three-time widow finally gave up on Rood in 1918 and married U.S. naval commander Mark St. Clair Ellis. The brief union soon dissolved because of another woman and a lawsuit, according to Lena. She provided no further details but did not divorce him until 1932.

Lena bought a villa in the picturesque lakeside resort of Stresa, Italy, where she lived in virtual seclusion for nearly twenty years. For the seven dogs that kept her company, she built a private dining room, purchased a car, and hired a chauffeur. Upon her death, a strange note was found among her papers that read, "Today I refused to become Queen of Serbia." Her acquaintances included Peter I, the widowed king of Serbia, who may have proposed to the wealthy dowager at one time. Over the years, Lena apparently retained the special "something" that appealed to men, much like female black widow spiders that repel everything else but still attract their mates.

Perhaps a clue to the lady's sex appeal (for some Victorian men, at least) can be found in a 1910 interview Lena gave to a New York newspaper. Most Denver women were proud that Colorado had been the first state where men actually voted in favor of woman's suffrage in 1893. In the interview, Lena suggested instead that members of her sex (herself included) were too dimwitted to vote. Apparently the former "Captain Jack" turned into a helpless featherbrain whenever a man crossed her path, unless of course he happened to be a neighbor. Said Stoiber:

> In my opinion, in Colorado the right to vote is exercised to a large extent only among the poorer classes and among that class whose vote can be influenced by a free ride to the polls in an automobile. Of course there are some women of position who do vote, but a large proportion are of the strong-minded variety. The really feminine women as a rule are content to leave the governing to men.

At her death Lena divided the huge estate between her brother-in-law and sister, but other claimants came forth to challenge the will. Mark St. Clair Ellis protested that Lena owed him $136,000 on a promissory note, a claim that was later rejected. Curiously, a woman named Magdalena Dominiguez from Lena's hometown in Missouri purported to be her adopted daughter, backing up the story with a notation in a bible dated 1891 and signed by both Lena and Edward Stoiber. Dominiguez could never prove the relationship to the court's satisfaction, and after ten years and several reversals, Stoiber's brother received the bulk of the estate. Vain to the end, Lena made a special bequest of $10,000 to Sadie Freenor, a former hairdresser who had once told her that she was pretty.

### ❦
# For Love and Money
*Mollie O'Bryan*

*A* modern career woman in a nineteenth-century mining town, Mollie O'Bryan was the only female broker to ever hold a seat on the highly competitive Cripple Creek Mining Exchange. Using her business contacts to obtain inside information on investments, by the age of twenty-three she had raised enough capital to pay the required $5,000 security bond and membership fee. Together with her business partner, Charles N. Miller, she made and lost a fortune trading stocks.

The entrepreneurial Mollie (Mary E.) came to Colorado from Missouri with her family in the 1880s, while still a youngster. Working as a secretary in Lake City, she learned the mining and brokerage business before joining the stampede to Cripple Creek in 1893. As a stenographer with an office in the heart of the financial district, the attractive and outgoing young woman met a number of businessmen, investors, and mine owners, including Charles Miller.

Born in Buffalo, New York, Charles grew up in Pennsylvania, where he first learned the mining and brokerage business. Good looking and fast-talking, he relocated to Colorado Springs in 1892 and worked in several businesses, creating profits for others while making modest gains himself.

Hoping to start his own brokerage firm, he moved to Cripple Creek in 1894. He and Mollie immediately formed a close business and personal relationship, which didn't stop Charles from marrying socialite Josephine Cox of Colorado Springs the following year. Miller built his wife one of Cripple Creek's most spectacular homes while Mollie helped him create a financial empire.

According to historian Brian Levine in *Cripple Creek Gold*, Mollie's career as a wheeler-dealer took off when she invested in the Damon Gold Mining Company, purchasing $5 blocks of 1,000 shares over a period of several days. When the Damon stock reached 10 cents a share, she sold out and reinvested in other property, often quadrupling her money by using insider information that would be considered illegal today.

In December 1895, Mollie and Charles formed a syndicate with three other partners named Burbridge, Macrorie, and Young. By 1900, they owned and operated several financially successful mining companies, including the Teutonic and Transvaal. Miller became vice president of the Cripple Creek Mining Stock Exchange while Mollie opened a new downtown office, working as stenographer/broker/mine owner. They made a handsome pair, but Charles stayed married and Mollie stayed single. After their roller-coaster rides together on the market, perhaps she found other men a little dull.

In 1903, Mollie and Charles consolidated their holdings into a new organization called the Amalgamated Gold Mining Company. Unfortunately, they embarked upon the venture just in time for the Great Labor Wars of 1903–4, which shut down many companies. The Amalgamated never recovered. In 1909, Miller left Cripple Creek and Mollie for San Francisco's greener pastures, gaining some measure of success with another brokerage company that dealt in copper mines. Mollie remained in Cripple Creek, still struggling along as a stenographer/broker and living with her sister. She died of a cerebral hemorrhage on December 30, 1922, at age forty-nine.

## 🎵

# Passion and Politics
*Goldie Mabovitch (Golda Meir)*
*and Morris Meyerson*

*A* classic attraction of opposites, the love match between a high spirited Jewish teenager named Goldie Mabovitch and the quiet young intellectual known as Morris Meyerson blossomed in Denver shortly before World War I. Although their relationship faltered long before Goldie changed her name to Golda Meir and became Israel's prime minister, Morris always held a special place in her heart as her first love. Years later, she would fondly recall their courtship and romantic summer concerts in the park, where the couple would hold hands and sit spellbound by the strains of Liszt's *Second Hungarian Rhapsody* or Giuseppi Verdi's *Il Travatore*. "To this day," she wrote, "I associate certain pieces of music with the clear, dry mountain air of Denver and the wonderful parks in which Morris and I walked every Sunday in the spring and summer of 1914."

Both Goldie and Morris were immigrants to the United States. Goldie was born in Kiev, Russia, in May 1893, the daughter of a carpenter named Moshe Mabovitch. Although Mabovitch was a skilled craftsman, the family suffered extreme poverty. In nineteenth-century Russia, the Jews faced terrible persecution and lived in constant fear of mass executions called pogroms. As a child Goldie once witnessed a group of Cossacks on horseback galloping over Jewish youngsters playing in the street, a terrifying image that she never forgot.

The family fled to the United States in 1908 and settled in Milwaukee, Wisconsin. Moshe found sporadic employment in railroad workshops, while Goldie's mother, Bluma,

Goldie Mabovitch would leave her first love behind to become Israeli prime minister and world leader Golda Meir. *(Courtesy of the Golda Meir Museum, Auraria Higher Education Center)*

opened a grocery store in the vacant shop adjacent to their tiny flat. Although Goldie was a brilliant student who loved school, Bluma took a dim view of education for women. Conflict escalated when Goldie graduated from grade school as class valedictorian and expressed the desire to go to high school and become a teacher. Since Milwaukee law forbade teachers to marry, her parents were horrified—the proper Jewish girl was expected to marry young and begin a family immediately. When Goldie's mother found a potential husband, a Mr. Ralph Goodstein, who sold insurance and was twice her age, the rebellious fifteen-year-old ran away from home. After scrawling a simple farewell note to her parents ("I am going to live with Sheyna so I can study,") she slipped out of the house and caught a train heading west to join her older sister, who had sent her the money.

While Goldie took destiny into her own hands, Morris Meyerson's life had been dictated by circumstance. His family immigrated to the United States from Lithuania when he was twelve, and shortly afterward his father died. Morris worked to support the family during the day and took classes at night, a tireless student with a great love of music. When his sister Sarah contracted tuberculosis, Morris moved his mother and all three sisters to Denver, where he worked intermittently as a sign painter. He later met Goldie through Sheyna, Sarah's roommate at the National Jewish Hospital.

As Golda states in her 1975 autobiography, "In Denver, life really opened up for me, although Sheyna and Sam (Shamai) proved to be almost as strict as my parents and we all had to work very hard." After school, Goldie helped earn her keep as a presser at Sam's dry cleaning establishment, Korngold's Cleaning and Pressing Works, at 18th and Curtis Streets near the Brown Palace Hotel.

Sheyna and Sam had always been political activists. Their small apartment became a gathering place for Russian Jewish immigrants, who had come for treatment at Denver's famous Jewish Hospital for Consumptives. Some were anarchists, some were socialists, and some were Zionists, but all were passionately and vitally concerned with the major issues of the day. Goldie listened with rapt attention and volunteered to disinfect the cups afterward.

"I think I first noticed Morris because, although he was almost entirely self-educated, he was so well versed in the kind of things that neither I nor most of Sheyna and Shamai's friends knew anything at all about," Golda said later. "He loved poetry, art and music and knew and understood a great deal about them, and he was prepared to talk at length on the merits of a given sonnet or sonata to someone as interested (and as ignorant) as I was."

As Goldie blossomed into a lovely young woman who enjoyed male company, her sister became even more overbearing. After a particularly bitter quarrel about her late dates, Goldie stormed out of the house one night and moved in with friends, both seriously ill with tuberculosis. Eventually she found her own tiny apartment, a daring move for a sixteen-year-old girl in 1913. Forced to quit school, she got a job at a laundry, where she stretched curtains. She also worked at the Denver Dry Goods Store as a seamstress, taking measurements for custom hemlines. During this period, Morris played Professor Higgins to her Eliza Doolittle, providing her with long reading lists and piles of books. Since they had little money, they attended free lectures and music performances or went boating at Sloan's Lake.

After a year on her own, Goldie received a message from her father, warning her to "come home, if you value your mother's life." Since the family had relented and agreed that she could finish school, Goldie made plans to return to Milwaukee. Before she left for home, Morris told her that he loved her and asked her to marry him. She happily agreed, writing to her friend that "He isn't very handsome, but he has a beautiful soul."

Upon her return to Milwaukee, Goldie (now called Golda) became immersed in politics and joined the Zionist Party, a group that believed the Jews should have their own homeland in Palestine. A man more interested in poetry than politics, Morris responded negatively. "The other day I received a note to attend one of the [Zionist] meetings, but since I do not care particularly whether the Jews suffer in Russia or the Holy Land, I did not go. You get your Jewish state, so there'll be another country in the world. So what?"

The long-distance engagement somehow endured for three years. Golda meant to go to Palestine, but Morris wouldn't budge. Her political friends urged Golda to find someone else, but she was determined to win him over. In 1917, the British officially endorsed the establishment of a

Jewish state in Palestine and Golda informed Morris that she was going (the "with or without you" was undoubtedly understood). Morris reluctantly agreed to accompany her "as a wedding present" if she would marry him immediately. The couple wed on December 14, 1917, in her parents' dining room, attended by a small group of friends. Golda was nineteen and Morris twenty-four.

In 1921, the couple left the United States to immigrate to Israel. Golda later recalled, "I owed America much. I arrived a frightened little girl. When I left, I was not fleeing from oppression and insecurity. I was leaving of my own accord a good, generous people. I was born under a tyranny, but brought up in a democracy. I took what I valued with me."

Golda and Morris initially joined an agricultural collective called a kibbutz, where she finally overcame the stereotype of as a "soft American girl." In 1924, they moved to Tel Aviv, then Jerusalem, because Morris disapproved of collective child rearing and wanted Golda to become a full-time homemaker. She tried. During this period, Golda gave birth to two children, Menahem and Sarah, but she was miserable away from the political arena. Determined to do her part in building the nation, she would later become one of the signers of Israel's Declaration of Independence. Her dedication put a strain on the marriage, which steadily disintegrated as she gained celebrity, power, and position. They separated in 1928.

Golda took many lovers over the next several years. Politically dynamic men such as David Remez and Zalam

Shazar shared her goals and vision and bolstered her career. She never remarried, partly because Morris refused to give her a divorce and partly because some of her lovers were already married. Most important, she never met anyone else she wanted to marry. In her autobiography, Golda maintains that she cared for Morris until he died in 1951 (symbolically, while she was out of the country). "The tragedy wasn't that he didn't understand me, but that he understood me too well. I had to be what I was, and what I was made it impossible for him to have the sort of wife he wanted or needed."

Friends and comrades always wondered why she had married a man so different in temperament and character, who never shared her robust passion for life and dedication to politics. When asked, she simply smiled and responded softly, "Because I loved him."

❧

## COURTSHIP ON WHEELS

During the late 1890s, women's newly aroused interest in sports, particularly bicycling, gave the courting couple a break from the confines of the parlor and a taste of freedom. One of the most bicycle-friendly cities in the country, Denver boasted four cyclists per ten residents. The city became a regional hub for the sport, with numerous clubs, bicycle stores, and even a weekly magazine called *Cycling West*. Unlike many parts of the country overly concerned about propriety, Colorado encouraged women cyclists. Physicians maintained that riding a bicycle provided good exercise, although young women were advised to abandon their corsets and wear shorter skirts for a more comfortable ride. Not everyone agreed on the propriety of made-to-order bicycle attire, however. In 1903, piano teacher Mamie Young (whose pupils included Molly Brown's nieces) scandalized the old Auraria neighborhood by riding around in a split skirt.

Etiquette manuals, books, and magazines provided behavioral guidelines for young cyclists. "Learn the art of the bicycle mount," advised feminist Frances E Willard. "The gentleman accompanying the lady holds her wheel; she stands at the left, places her right foot across the frame to the right pedal, which at the same time must be raised. Pushing this pedal causes the machine to start, and then with the left foot in place she starts ahead, very slowly in order to give her companion time to mount his wheel and join her. When their destination is reached, the gentleman dismounts first and appears at his companion's side to assist her; if she be a true American woman, she will assist herself as much as possible."

Cycling provided many opportunities for spontaneous flirting and secret trysts as the following poem suggests.

### Proposal on Wheels

*Along upon their wheels they spun, he close near her side,*
*She a brief-skirted maiden, one he fain would make his bride.*
*He reached and took her hand in his, gave it a loving squeeze*
*The while his warmth of passion riz a whole lot of degrees.*

*He cried: My love consumeth me. My breast is all on fire,*
*'Tis love as boundless as the sea, Love that can never "tire."*
*See how my "frame" is all convulsed with signs I can't conceal,*
*If my advances are repulsed to ruin I will wheel.*

*I do not "pedal" out my love to every girl I meet,*
*As peddlers hawk their wares who rove along the busy street.*
*Think not I am a "crank," or that my brain is out of gear,*
*Or that I'm talking through my hat, I'm honest and sincere.*

*If you should scorn my honest plea how sad'll be my lot.*
*No hand'll bar my misery from being overwrought.*
*But if to hear me you will deign, and take me for your "hub,"*
*How smooth will run affection's "chain" without a jar or rub.*

*The maiden raised a warning hand and bade him pause awhile,*
*Said she would have him understand that chains were out of style.*
*She told him he had better go and seek another dove,*
*She'd find a fellow who'd bestow on her a chainless love.*

*Cycling West*, February 3, 1898

## ❧
# All the World Is a Stage
### *Mary Rippon and Will Housel*

*A* soft breeze ripples through the pines on a balmy summer evening as playgoers take their seats for the annual Shakespeare Festival. Behind the stage, actors dressed in tights, togas, and sometimes T-shirts prepare for the performance. As the play begins, the poet's lyrical phrases drift through the courtyard of the Mary Rippon Theater, a University of Colorado landmark since 1936. The 1,200-seat theater was lovingly, if ironically, dedicated to the CU's pioneering female professor, who paved the way for Colorado women in higher education.

The university regents unknowingly chose the perfect monument to honor Mary Rippon, who put on a stellar performance during the greater part of her career. While presenting herself as a sedate spinster and a paragon of Victorian female virtue, Mary led a bizarre double life that would have scandalized the establishment and fascinated the Bard himself. Even more amazing, she managed to keep marriage and motherhood a secret for more than fifty years beyond her own lifetime.

Mary's unusual personal background may account for some of her choices. Born on May 25, 1850, to Thomas and

Jane Rippon, she lost her father before her first birthday. Because Rippon died without a will, Illinois state law dictated that his property should go to Mary, his only child, rather than his wife, Jane. The court placed the estate, including 166 acres of prime farmland, into a trust until Mary turned eighteen. Since Jane had no means of support, Mary's grandfather (on her mother's side) became the child's legal guardian. After three years Jane married Norman Whitney and the couple had a son. When Jane's father died, the court transferred guardianship to her brother, William.

When Mary was six, Jane petitioned for a "widow's right of dower," or ownership of one-third of the farm. William intervened with the court on the child's behalf and forced a sale, depositing the proceeds back into Mary's trust. Short of funds and without a home, Norman moved Jane and Mary's half-brother to Kansas, leaving the little girl behind with a neighboring family. Although Mary received excellent care and education, separation from her mother and brother must have been traumatic. Jane died nine years later, probably without ever seeing her daughter again.

Mary's Uncle William worked to increase her inheritance and made sure that she understood the importance of money and financial management. With a benevolent guardian and a trust fund to pay for her education, the bright young woman went on to high school at Illinois State Normal School. When she turned eighteen, the court awarded her the equivalent of $40,000, and she took off to explore Europe with a chaperoned study group.

Since Europeans were somewhat more enlightened than Americans about women in higher education, Mary studied at the University of Hanover in Germany and the University of Paris, although she never obtained a college degree. At twenty-seven, she returned to Illinois a culturally sophisticated young woman with an impressive command of German and French. After teaching high school in Detroit for two years, she received a job offer from Dr. Joseph Sewall, a teacher she had met at the high school. Recently appointed the first president of the fledgling University of Colorado at Boulder, Sewell invited her to join him at the new institution. Mary arrived in January 1878 to become the school's third faculty member. At the time, the tuition-free University of Colorado consisted of a single three-story red brick building on an open prairie, with a student body of forty-four young men and women. Sewell set a high moral and educational standard for the new college, and made his expectations clear to everyone.

Mary had a knack for teaching and a winning personality. Attractive in a lithe, energetic sort of way, she stood five feet six inches, with fair skin, brown hair, and a pretty oval face. Because of her personal assets, she could afford to dress well, albeit without frills. Boulderites were impressed by her background and experience, and she loved the landscape, which she said reminded her of the Swiss Alps. By spring 1881, she had been promoted to full professor and named chair of the modern languages department. Although she made a respectable salary, she still earned less than male colleagues. Adored by her students and the community, she wrote in her diary that she still felt lonely at times.

In 1887, Will Housel came into Mary's life and led her happily astray. At twenty-five, Housel looked like the ideal of nineteenth-century Teutonic masculinity, with dark eyes that reflected sensitivity and passion; a wide, full-lipped mouth; and a muscular physique typical of German men, who took exercise quite seriously. A perennial student born into a well-educated Boulder farming family, he enrolled in Mary's German grammar and literature class and they developed a close friendship. Mary often gave her students individual attention, but her relationship with Will led to an incredibly risky affair, at least on her part. With a successful career dependent on her suitability as a role model for young women, she fell head over heels for a student twelve years her junior, who still lived with his parents!

When Mary realized she was pregnant she asked for a sabbatical, supposedly to recover after a bout with respiratory illness and neuralgia. At thirty-eight, she had no illusions that she could continue teaching after giving birth to an illegitimate child. Even if she married Will, she would be forced to resign and her affair with a student would make her an academic pariah. Still, the lovers chose to be together, at least for a while. When the spring term ended in June 1888, she and Will took separate trains to Saint Louis, where they were married. After a month-long "honeymoon" with her aunt and uncle in Illinois, Will returned to Boulder and Mary took a steamer to join a close friend in Germany. In January, she gave birth to a baby girl, who she named Miriam Edna Housel. After Will graduated the following spring, he joined Mary and the baby in Switzerland.

In a decision totally alien to any notion of Victorian propriety, the couple determined that Will should remain in Europe to continue his education and watch over their daughter, who was placed in a Catholic orphanage. Mary returned to Colorado to resume her career and support the family, earning extra money through interest-bearing loans to fellow faculty members and students. In 1891, Will temporarily gave up his educational pursuit and returned to Boulder to help his father on the farm, leaving the little girl in Europe. Once in Boulder, he visited his wife once or twice a week. Mary's pristine reputation left them remarkably free from gossip. Although a few close friends knew of the relationship, somehow they kept quiet. Mary supported her husband in numerous ventures, providing a down payment on his father's farm and helping him purchase an agricultural newspaper, the *Colorado Farmer and Livestock Journal.* At one point she was giving half her salary to Will while still supporting their daughter overseas.

The unconventional marriage must have been a strain, but Mary could not (or would not) give up her career. They wrangled with the problem for nearly two years. In 1893, the couple arranged for Miriam's passage to the United States, where she was introduced to "Aunt Mary," at the Chicago World's Fair. That fall, Will moved to Ann Arbor, Michigan, and enrolled in graduate school, taking the child along. Mary and Will must have divorced at some point, but the legal proceedings were as surreptitious as the marriage.

In June 1896, Will married a young Connecticut woman named Dora Mae Searles. Although she may have felt uncomfortable in the role, Mary served as babysitter for her "niece" at a seaside resort while the couple went on their honeymoon. Over the years, she continued to send child support and often gave money to Will, who never could earn a living. Finally, Mary bought a farm in Ann Arbor for the family, which eventually included two little boys and a baby girl. She supported Will's brood for years, taking trips back and forth from Michigan to visit and help with expenses. Why Mary chose to pay her ex-husband's way through life remains a mystery. Perhaps she still loved him and wanted to continue some kind of relationship, or maybe she felt guilty for leaving him alone to raise their daughter. If blackmail were the case (emotional or otherwise), Mary could simply have sent a check—she certainly didn't need to take Will's wife out shopping! Meanwhile, Miriam still had no inkling that generous "Aunt Mary" was really her mother.

After two decades of dedication and deception, Mary Rippon found herself physically, financially, and emotionally exhausted. She retired in 1909 with the help of an endowment from the Carnegie Foundation and moved in with her daughter in Wisconsin while the girl attended college. Mary continued to visit Will almost every summer until he was killed in a motorcycle accident in 1912, just six months after the death of his second wife.

Miriam learned of her father's first marriage and her true parentage a few years later, during final settlement of his affairs. She did not take the news well, if she believed it at all. Miriam rarely talked about Mary in later years and certainly never referred to her as "my mother." She spoke fondly of Will, but never mentioned her stepmother and stepbrothers, whom she apparently resented. After her divorce from a German professor with Nazi sympathies, Miriam took a teaching position at the University of Colorado. The women continued their "aunt-niece" relationship until Mary died in 1935.

Miriam never divulged the secret publicly, although her son, Wilfred Reider, knew the truth. In 1987, half a century after Mary's death, an elderly man walked into the university archives to donate two photographs, and later passed along some of Mary's journals and diaries. Even after nearly a century, he shocked the entire community by identifying himself as Mary Rippon's grandson.

## ⚓

# Adventurer in the Sun-Land
*Verner Z. Reed*

*V*erner Z. Reed had the soul of a poet and the instincts of a used-car salesman. He could write steamy romances that titillated Victorian dowagers, yet he made a fortune during Cripple Creek's boom days in that most unromantic of professions—real estate. With a zest for life worthy of a Renaissance prince, he made his mark as a businessman, writer, explorer, and philanthropist. And when he died in 1919, he was worth more than $120 million in today's currency.

A self-educated man, Verner came from a family of thirteen children. Born in Ohio and raised on an Iowa farm, he helped his father support the family while still a youngster. Verner's literary talent came in handy after he moved to Colorado Springs in 1885 and began writing promotional brochures for tourists. Always an entrepreneur, he soon expanded operations and opened his own real estate business, plotting and selling lots in the city. When the gold boom struck nearby Cripple Creek in 1893, Reed found his niche as the town's biggest promoter. Conveniently, one of his best friends, former carpenter Winfield Stratton, had become king of the new mining giants. When Stratton sold his beloved Independence Mine to the London Venture Corporation, Reed pocketed a million-dollar commission.

While Verner Reed was getting rich, he relaxed by writing novels and short stories. A combination Ernest Hemingway and Danielle Steele, he spent a great deal of time researching the Ute and Pueblo Indians, often in the company of artist and ex-Indian scout Charles Craig. According to rumor, he based the stories on his own experiences. Reed loved to tell friends how he nearly collapsed from exhaustion after a four-day bear dance with a Native American girl. This revelation must have appalled his conservative wife, the former Mary Dean Johnson, daughter of a prominent Colorado Springs realtor.

*Lo-To-Kah* and *Tales of the Sun-Land*, Verner's first two books, were considered quite racy when they were published in 1897. His stories have a romantic mystical quality that curiously combines empathy with condescension toward Native Americans and Hispanics. The following passage, passionate but hardly erotic by today's standards, is taken from the story "The Carib Queen" in *Tales of the Sun-Land*:

> Before we knew it, I and the golden queen were plighted lovers. I do not remember how many days went by before I took her in my arms and told her she was all the world to me. I only know that it was natural for us to love each other—as natural as it is for the flowers to bloom in the light of the sun. When her arms were clasped about me and her lips pressed to mine, I knew a happiness that few men know this side of heaven.

The following is a sexier excerpt from the same book, a ghost story called "An Enchanted Night":

> She pressed her lips to mine and seemed to drink in
> my very breath, and as she kissed me her form
> expanded into perfect womanhood. Her fair propor-
> tions, delicately molded, were yet as strong as steel; her
> breast rose and fell in ecstasy and her eyes sparkled
> with the light of love. The very elements seemed to
> grow beautiful with her; perfume floated with the air,
> and soft sounds, like the strains of distant music, fell
> upon the hearing. She twined her rounded arms about
> me and from then I took no heed of time.

To write his third book, *Adobeland Stories*, Reed went to
Europe and stayed six years. He took a few side trips to the
Middle East, enjoying (or enduring) one of the first automo-
tive caravans across the Sahara. A philanthropist and
humanitarian by nature, he favored labor unions, and when
World War I broke out, President Wilson appointed him to
mediate labor-management conflicts around the country.

By the time Reed's hard drinking caught up with him
around 1918, he and Mary were living separately. With his
son, Verner Jr., and his best friend, Father David O'Dwyer, he
traveled to California, where he died at Coronado Beach on
April 20, 1919. In accordance with Reed's wishes, his widow
distributed millions to charities around the state. Despite her
generosity, Mary Dean Reed, known locally as "the Lady
Bountiful," had a keen business sense and added another $6
million to the Reed estate before her death in 1945.

## 🦢

# **The Magnificent Margaret Brown**
*Maggie and J. J. Brown*

*A*long with the notorious Baby Doe Tabor, Margaret Tobin Brown is probably Colorado history's best-known female celebrity. Dubbed "unsinkable" by *Denver Post* reporter Polly Pry, Maggie Brown (who was never called Molly during her lifetime) became an international heroine in 1912, when the ocean liner *Titanic* sank after hitting an iceberg. By rallying lifeboat passengers and encouraging them to row to safety, she demonstrated remarkable courage and tenacity. When the rescue ship *Carpathia* docked in New York City, the flamboyant Maggie already had become a legend, surrounded by journalists and admirers eager to hear her account of the tragedy. (She had a talent for self-promotion that any modern rock star would admire.) Back in Denver, her estranged husband, J. J. Brown, grumbled to a friend, "She's too mean to sink."

For obvious reasons, the story of Maggie's stormy marriage to J. J. Brown generally takes a backseat to the *Titanic* adventure. Still, their relationship was a passionate love match, and it made all the difference in her life. After he died, a young reporter questioned Maggie about Brown, from whom she had been separated for more than a decade. "I've never met a finer, bigger,

Husband J. J. threatened to shoot *Titanic* heroine
Margaret (Molly) Brown when their marriage
went on the rocks. *(Courtesy of the Colorado
Historical Society, #F-8098)*

more worthwhile man than J. J. Brown," she responded with
dignity. "In spite of certain qualities of our nature that made
companionship impossible between us, I salute his memory and
claim him to be without peer." When asked if she would ever

consider remarriage, Maggie seemed shocked. "My dear! How can you ask such a question after what I just told you?"

Margaret Tobin met James Joseph Brown at a church picnic in the early summer of 1886. Recently arrived from Hannibal, Missouri, she came to Leadville with her half-brother, Daniel, to join other relatives in the town's Irish Catholic community. While Daniel toiled in the mines for $2.50 a day, Maggie cooked her brother's meals and sewed drapes for the Daniels, Fisher and Smith Department Store. (Later she told friends that she put on "penny shows" with songs and poetry recitals for miners in the evenings.) Poor and uneducated, the well-built redhead hoped to improve her status by snagging a wealthy husband who could help support her ailing father back in Hannibal.

Brown was thirteen years older than Maggie, big-boned, blue-eyed, and devastatingly attractive to women. He grew up in Pennsylvania, and then headed west at age twenty-three to try his luck at mining. A self-trained geologist with a talent for sniffing out ore deposits, he easily found a job as shift manager for the mining interests of David Moffat and Eben Smith, then worked himself up to superintendent of the valuable Maid and Henriette Mine. Although he earned a respectable middle-class salary, Maggie doubted that J. J. could ever provide the luxuries she wanted. According to a family story, she refused to go out with him when he arrived for their first date in a shabby, one-horse carriage. (Abashed, he returned the next evening in a fancier rig.) Eventually, his Irish charm won her over. "I decided that I'd be better off with a poor man whom I loved than a wealthy one whose money attracted me," she later admitted to a reporter. After a brief courtship, they married on September 1, 1886.

The early years were the happiest. The young couple moved into J. J.'s small two-room cabin in Stumptown, where Maggie embarked on a career as a not-so-typical Victorian housewife. With an eye toward self-improvement, she began taking lessons in reading, literature, and music in Leadville. Life in the old mining camp was fairly primitive. The town had no sidewalks, one road, and a single pump from which to draw water, unless folks were willing to use the creek. With only coal or wood-burning stoves for heat and no electricity, mountain winters were harsh, cold, and dark. Everyone used outhouses and bathed in washtubs, since indoor plumbing and a sewage system were luxuries reserved for city folks. During the next three years, Maggie and J. J. had two children, Lawrence Palmer in 1888 and Catherine Ellen in 1889. Some gossips whispered that Brown strayed occasionally, but at least he remained discreet.

After several years of moderate financial success, they hit the jackpot at the Little Jonny Mine. Brown purchased stock in the Ibex Mining Co., which owned the Little Jonny. When the price of silver plummeted in 1893, J. J. decided to work the mine for gold instead of silver. People stopped calling him a fool when he hit pay dirt with a pure, wide vein of gold and rejuvenated the town's economy.

Like many Leadville millionaires, the Browns moved to Denver as soon as possible. In the elite Capitol Hill district they purchased a relatively modest home at 1340 Pennsylvania Street, flanked by two stone lions and furnished with all the latest conveniences. Maggie brought her father to Colorado, along with several other relatives. While J. J. expanded his mining interests and hired several of his wife's kin, Maggie set out to impress Denver's social dragons. Although her Irish Catholic background precluded membership in Louise Hill's Sacred 36 (the Mount Everest of Denver society), Maggie's name appeared frequently in the newspapers as she became active in fund-raising for many charitable causes, including Judge Ben Lindsey's juvenile court. Despite her good works, snippy reporters considered her a publicity-happy social climber. "Perhaps no woman in society has ever spent more time or money becoming civilized than Mrs. Brown," one *Denver Times* critic wrote sarcastically. In a later article, the *Times* reflected that "Social leadership requires more than the ability to pay a good chef and the taste to select a clever dressmaker."

Undaunted, Maggie took French lessons, traveled abroad, sent her children to expensive schools in France and England, and generously spread her husband's money around Europe. Eventually, her need to be the constant center of attention wore on J. J.'s Victorian sensibilities (he must have been mortified when she took up yodeling and performed in public at Elitch Gardens). Decked out in feather boas, large hats, and heavily beaded Parisian gowns, she usually stole the show at social events. On one occasion she wore her hair à la Marie Antoinette, with a gilt snake coiled around a headpiece that flashed two large solitaires and a cluster of opals and diamonds. Her jewelry collection alone would have fetched about $850,000 in today's currency.

Weary of his wife's soirees, Brown often retreated to another part of the house to smoke and drink with his father-in-law while Maggie entertained. He did accompany her to social affairs, and they both enjoyed the theater. After J. J. suffered a stroke in 1899, the family announced plans to move permanently to Ireland, but they were back in Denver before the end of the year. The couple grew even farther apart after Maggie enrolled for a year's study in 1901 at New York's Carnegie Institute. When she came home for Christmas, a major scandal erupted when an irate Harry D. Call, who worked for gold baron W. S. Stratton, sued Brown for seducing his twenty-two-year-old wife. Described by one newspaper as a tall blonde with a splendid figure and laughing eyes, Maude Morton Call met J. J. at a Pueblo health resort and subsequently abandoned her family in the hopes of taking their liaison a step further. To patch things up, J. J. took Maggie on a 'round-the-world tour, including Egypt, India, and Japan.

During the next few years J. J. spent a lot of time out of town, and the pair were seldom seen in public together. With a good deal of bitterness, they finally separated in 1909. Maggie testified in court that her husband was "given to periods of moroseness, with an insane desire to kill me … He tried twice. I got the gun both times while he wept and afterward cried, begging me to go away where he could not kill me." Although she may have fabricated the attempted shootings, no one doubted that J. J. wanted her to leave. Stung, she tried to turn the children against him and hid his letters from them. "Your mother is my worst enemy," he told his son.

In the separation agreement, Maggie received a small cash settlement, their house on Pennsylvania Street, and an allowance of $700 a month to continue her travels. Still, she quarreled with J. J. continuously. They may have missed one another, but Irish tempers, stubbornness, and mutual paranoia made reconciliation impossible. Brown accused Maggie of following him because she wanted more money, while Maggie thought J. J. was trailing her because he wanted a divorce. At one point Brown did consider hiring a private detective to prove his wife insane, a contention occasionally supported by their daughter. Meanwhile, Maggie became more outspoken in her political beliefs and even ran twice (unsuccessfully) for the U.S. Senate. As Denver's first historic preservationist, she saved the Eugene Field house, which she then bullied the city into moving to Washington Park. (A well-known humorist, poet, and author of children's verse, Field lived briefly in Denver while working as a journalist for the *Denver Times*.)

J. J. spent his sunset years in hospitals and sanitariums, reflecting sadly on the good days in Leadville and the ambitious redhead he'd won and lost. He died in their daughter's home in 1922. Little remained of his estate due to all those years of high living, but Maggie and the children quarreled over what remained. Estranged from her family, Maggie divided her time between the Saint James Hotel in Paris and the Barbizon Hotel in New York City, a gathering place for aspiring young actresses. Long enamored of Sarah Bernhardt, whom she'd met in Denver, Maggie received international recognition for her impersonation of the famous actress. She occasionally performed Bernhardt's roles for charity benefits. Although Denverites still considered her crude, European royalty and American socialites such as the Astors and Vanderbilts appreciated her quick wit. She continued traveling, and studied and taught acting until 1932, when she died of a cerebral hemorrhage. Reconciled with her former husband in death (as she never could be in life) Maggie lies next to J. J. in Long Island's Holy Rood Cemetery. Their former residence at 1340 Pennsylvania Street has been preserved as one of Denver's finest house museums.

### CHAPTER VI

# Haunting Romances

## The Lady of the Columbines

*John Cameron's Mourner*

When the November wind sweeps the crinkled leaves around the old Central City Masonic cemetery, a young woman climbs the hillside toward a weathered gravesite. Dressed in a long black satin brocade dress with wildflowers pinned in her hair, she might have stepped out of an antique portrait. For a few moments she stands silent next to a vine-covered marble headstone and kneels to place a fresh bouquet of blue columbines on the grave. As evening approaches she slips away, a legendary phantom from Central's halcyon days.

Tales of the mysterious lady of the columbines materialized in 1887, with the death of the town's most eligible gentleman. John Edward Cameron had been one of Central's favorite sons, a pleasant young man whose passing left the entire town in mourning. John's parents were transplanted Canadians of Scottish descent who moved to Gilpin County from Nebraska in 1866. Young Cameron grew up in Central City, where his natural charm and generosity made him popular around town. Like many strong young men, he joined Central's Rescue, Fire, and Hose Company #1, and he soon received a promotion to first assistant foreman. After John became a hero by rescuing miners from a cave-in, several young women tried valiantly to rescue *him* from bachelorhood. Local belles showered him with social invitations and home cooking, but he usually attended parties in the company of his male friends. When attempts failed to engage his affections long-term, someone started the rumor that he already had a lover. Folks surmised that she must live somewhere near Bald Mountain or Nevadaville, where he often took long walks on summer evenings.

On November 1, 1887, Cameron's sudden demise left the town's marriageable women grasping for the smelling salts. According to an article in Central's *Register-Call*, John had fallen ill on the previous day from a mysterious malady. He had been sitting at home by the window when suddenly he called out to his mother and collapsed from what the doctor called "paralysis of the heart." He was barely twenty-eight years old when he died. Services held at the First Presbyterian Church left standing room only as friends and comrades delivered respectful eulogies and many maidenly tears were shed. An elegant procession to the Masonic Cemetery led by the Gilpin County Reed and Brass Band provided the deceased with a gallant farewell.

After the funeral, a mysterious young woman in mourning dress remained by the gravesite after everyone had left. She returned nearly every day and brought an armful of columbines and wild roses in April. No one saw her again after June, but she reappeared two years later in November on the anniversary of John's death. For the next ten years, the woman returned periodically in November or April, dressed in the same black satin brocade of the 1880s. No one could identify her or get close enough to talk. A few of the town's more imaginative souls decided that she was a ghost, a sentiment pooh-poohed by the town fathers. (Symbolically, Central City's fortunes began to decline about the same time. Although Gilpin County still led the state in gold production, mines were slowly playing out in the "richest square mile on earth." By 1893, discovery of the elusive metal in Cripple Creek left Central in the dust, a shadow of the boomtown made famous by John Gregory's strike.)

On November 1, 1899, fourteen people gathered at the Masonic Cemetery to solve the mystery of John Cameron's visitor once and for all. Near sunset they gathered by the gate as the lady made an appearance from the opposite side of the cemetery. Moving in a mist toward the grave, she placed a bouquet near the tombstone, spoke a few words that no one could understand, and silently moved away. Some of the onlookers tried to follow, but she disappeared over the crest of the hill. A terrific, eerie wind arose from the same direction, forcing the former cynics to "give up the ghost," and return to town. No one could explain how the lady managed to escape, since she had no place to hide.

During the next few decades the columbine lady occasionally reappeared again in April or November, but her identity remained a mystery. Some maintained that she was John's secret sweetheart, whom he had planned to marry in April. Others suggested that John died of a broken heart after she spurned him (à la Sweet William and Barbara Allen in the folk song), and that the lady haunted his grave out of guilt and remorse. The only person who may have known the stranger's identity was Cameron's mother, Catherine, who refused to discuss the matter. She took the secret to her grave in 1912, when she was buried next to her husband and son.

Sightings of the mysterious lady have been infrequent during the past few decades, and it's hard to say exactly how those wild roses and columbines sometimes appear on John Cameron's grave. Still, when the November frost covers the sleepy hillside or the first buds of April pop out of the ground, Central City old-timers keep an eye out for a woman in a long black dress, sadly trudging up the mountain toward the Masonic Cemetery.

## 🐚
# Harrowing Hotel Hauntings

*E*ven before Colorado became a state in 1876, her snow-capped peaks and clear mountain air attracted travelers, adventurers, and health seekers. Despite the best efforts of Colorado promoters, however, the tourist industry got off to a slow start. During the 1858–59 gold rush, the only available accommodations were overnight stage stops and boomtown flophouses such as Denver's Eldorado Hotel. After the Civil War, early sightseers were often discouraged by the teeth-rattling stagecoach trek across the plains and over the mountains. Future president Grant traveled through Colorado in 1865, but wisely postponed subsequent visits until he could take the train.

After the railroads chugged into Colorado in the 1870s, luxurious hotels and grand resorts sprang up to cater to a blossoming tourist industry. Many of the state's older hostelries are still in operation, including the famous Stanley Hotel in Estes Park, the inspiration for Stephen King's horror novel *The Shining*. Others include the Strater Hotel in Durango, the Hotel Colorado in Glenwood Springs, the Hotel Boulderado in Boulder, and the Brown Palace and Oxford Hotel in Denver. These wonderful historic haunts provide the perfect backdrop for ghost stories, particularly those involving illicit liaisons, love gone wrong, or even murder.

**Homicide in Room 454**

The Glenwood Canyon region on the Western Slope blossomed as one of the state's first resorts in the 1880s, shortly after the Ute Indians were conveniently removed from the land. Walter Devereaux, a mining engineer who made his fortune in Aspen, set out to create the world's most luxurious spa in picturesque Glenwood Springs. He first built a 615-foot hot springs pool, which was enhanced by a Richardsonian Romanesque-style lodge and bathhouse. Next came the red sandstone and brick six-story hotel, modeled after a sixteenth-century Italian mansion called Villa di Medici. The elegant two-hundred-room hotel, which opened in 1893, became one of the first in the country to be lit entirely by electricity.

Glenwood Springs became a favorite haunt of the rich and socially prominent, including silver king Horace Tabor and his beautiful young wife, Baby Doe. Over the years, the Hotel Colorado welcomed everyone from the Astors and the Goulds to President Teddy Roosevelt, gangster Al Capone, and silent movie star Tom Mix.

During World War II, the Navy occupied the hotel and turned it into a hospital. According to local lore, a sexy young nurse named Bobbie (aka Roberta) amused herself during quiet moments by playing doctor with two naval officers. When they discovered her duplicity, one of her lovers bludgeoned her to death in Room 454. According to stories later told by hotel employees, the Navy hushed up the scandal, shipped the officers back to the front, and buried Roberta quietly in Linwood Cemetery somewhere near gunfighter Doc Holliday.

Terrified guests saw images of a blood-soaked body in Room 454 of the Glenwood Springs' Hotel Colorado. *(Courtesy of the Denver Public Library, Western History Collection, #H-216)*

After the war, guests staying in Room 454 would sometimes wake to a woman's terrified screams and images of a bloody body. This occurred frequently enough that the hotel converted the room into storage space. Occasionally, hotel employees and visitors will smell her perfume in the hallway or trailing from a certain table at Sunday brunch. Older patrons have identified the scent as "Gardenia," a perfume popular during the 1930s and 40s.

### The Demi-Ghost of the Delaware Hotel
The first stampede to Lake County took place during the 1860s, when hundreds of miners set up a camp at Oro City

near California Gulch. The gold boom fizzled quickly and the area remained desolate until the silver strike of 1877, which created Leadville. The Delaware block, built in 1886 by the three Callaway brothers, included one of the town's most elegant hotels. Named in honor of their home state, the hotel featured shops at the sidewalk level and fifty attractively furnished rooms upstairs.

Just three years after opening, the Delaware Hotel became the setting for a family spat that escalated into murder. A town not generally known for its squeamishness, even Leadville was appalled when a man named Jerry Coffey shot his wife twice in the back, presumably in front of their two children.

Ten years earlier, Boston-born Mary Gallagher had married a tall, fair-haired drifter named Jerry Coffey in Eureka, Nevada. In 1888, they moved to Colorado from Idaho with their two daughters. Although the Leadville community generally thought well of Mary, her husband had a reputation for drinking and troublemaking. The couple quarreled often and publicly, and in April 1889, Jerry Coffey had his wife arrested for adultery. He later retracted the accusations, but the following July, Mary had Coffey arrested for assault. When Officer John Morgan served the warrant, Coffey shot him twice, presumably without fatality. The hotheaded husband spent several weeks in the county jail, while Mary took up residence in the Delaware Hotel. When she became ill, she unwisely requested that her husband return to help with the girls.

On the morning of November 4, Mary returned to her room after visiting with a neighbor, Mrs. Robinson, to find

Jerry waiting in her room. He accused her of adultery again, they argued, and he grabbed for her throat. As she pulled away and ran for the door, Jerry drew a gun (the same one he had used on the officer) and shot her twice in the back. "I have been intending to kill you for a long time," he said calmly, putting on his boots and heading for the exit as she screamed for help. The captain of the police department apprehended him before he got out of the hotel. Mary told officers that she had "done no wrong," a statement validated by her neighbors and the hotel management. She explained that her husband had been "crazy with jealousy." As a defense, Coffey claimed that she had left the children alone to go to Room 8 with another man. "She harassed the life out of me," he cried. According to management, the room was an office that had been locked at the time.

"The brute displayed no evidence of insanity in this cold-blooded murder and the community will not stand any sentimental fuss over him in an attempt to save his worthless, wretched life," wrote the less-than-impartial *Leadville Democrat*. While Mr. Coffey cooled his heels in jail, his wife spent her last days paralyzed from the waist down. She died on November 7, with one bullet lodged in her spine and another in her abdomen. According to local lore, she still haunts the halls of the beautifully restored building outside Room 18, appearing only from the waist up.

### The Mysterious Caller on the Ninth Floor

Ohio carpenter Henry Cordes Brown made millions from real estate after coming to Denver in 1860. Always a visionary, he donated the land for the State Capitol and provided $1,000 for the city's first real library. He also built the city's most exclusive hotel on a triangular plot at Broadway, Tremont, and 17th Street, where he once grazed his cow. Brown spared no expense for his pet project, which was designed by architect Frank E. Edbrooke, using Colorado red granite and Arizona sandstone. Inside, the country's first atrium lobby rose eight floors above the ground, surrounded by cast-iron railings with elaborate grillwork panels. Imported white onyx graced the lobby, the Grand Salon on the second floor, and the eighth-floor ballroom. Originally the dining room, convention hall, and ballroom also were located on the eighth floor, which rose two stories and provided a spectacular view of the Rockies.

In 1937, the Brown Palace Hotel opened the Skyline Apartments, with elaborate suites for permanent residents. Society doyenne Louise Hill moved into one of the apartments in the late 1940s when failing health forced her to sell the Hill mansion at 9th and Sherman Streets. She stayed virtually secluded at the hotel until her death in 1955. Although her final years were quiet, Louise had been quite a mover in her younger days. For years she openly carried on a torrid affair with a mining engineer named Bulkeley Wells, despite the fact that both were married. (See "The Queen of Diamonds and the Jack of Hearts," Chapter III.)

Nearly a half-century later, the Brown Palace's historian, Julie Kanellos, began a series of "Affairs of the Heart" hotel tours, sharing stories about Mrs. Hill's interesting past. Almost immediately, the switchboard became inundated with calls from Room 904, where Mrs. Hill resided with her large staff of servants until her death. As log books reported, when the operators answered they heard only static on the line. These calls were doubly perplexing since an extensive renovation was underway on the eighth and ninth floors, and Louise's room had been stripped of furniture, carpets, wallpaper, lights, and a telephone. No telephone call could possibly have been made from the room, or any other on that floor, since all wiring had been removed.

The calls ceased when the details of Louise's amorous adventures were dropped from the tour.

Louise shares the Brown with several other spectral residents, including a train conductor and a formally dressed string quartet from the 1940s. Hotel guests occasionally report sounds of feminine laughter and chatter outside Room 801, which was originally part of the ballroom.

### ❧
## Spirits of
## the Castle Rock Brewery

*N*ewspapers during the late nineteenth and early twentieth
century had no qualms about mixing factual stories
with the fantastic or whimsical, even on the first few pages.
Tongue-in-cheek, the *Rocky Mountain News* recorded one
ghost story on November 14, 1874, about two spectral young
women, perhaps thwarted in love, who had been hanging
around the Castle Rock Brewery on the Rio Grande Railroad.
"They have indicated that they abandoned the flesh some
two years ago, but what their object in haunting the brewery
has not transpired," reported the *News*. "They make it
unpleasant for the hired man who sleeps in the brewery by
dropping in on him o' night." (The *News* did not speculate
about the possibility that the hired man might have been
sampling the wares.)

"Two flaming lights are carried by the specters, who are
decently dressed in black and white robes so long that they
trail several feet upon the floor. Occasionally, as for example
last Tuesday night, the place is filled with groans, which pro-
ceed from the apparitions as, with lights in hand, they flit
about the building like bats. John Harris, who lives with his
family in the neighborhood of the brewery, has often been

awakened by strange noises proceeding thereof." The *News* declared that it would no longer gratuitously insert notice of ghosts, since "They are becoming altogether too common and the denizens of the other world appear to be encouraged by the attention to make unduly frequent visits."

## ❧
# Weeping Bride of Glendale

Only a few crumbling walls remain of the old Glendale stage stop, destroyed by the great Pueblo flood of 1921. Once a prosperous way station between Colorado Springs, Cañon City, and Leadville, the station bustled with scores of passengers on their way to the mining camps during the Leadville gold and silver boom of the 1870s. Ordinary travelers mingled with gamblers, shady ladies, trappers, and speculators to provide a cosmopolitan atmosphere much like today's airports. A constellation of barns and corrals sheltered fresh horses for the stagecoaches and mules to accommodate prospectors bound for the mines. The stage stop was a key junction on the old Granite–Colorado City stagecoach route, built in 1873 by Bob Spotswood and William McClelland to service Colorado's most recent metallic merry-go-round. From Colorado City, now west Colorado Springs, the road followed the base of Cheyenne Mountain across the outlying plains to Glendale station, at the junction of Beaver and Red Creeks.

A gabled two-story ranch house of native gray stone, the stage stop sat on a grassy knoll above Beaver Creek. Constructed in the early 1860s by rancher J. H. McClure, who later financed Cañon City's Strathmore Hotel, the building also served as a community center. At the entrance, visitors were treated to the welcoming sight of two massive stone fire-places glowing in the large hall. A spiral staircase led to eleven bedrooms that provided plenty of sleeping space, although during peak periods bedrolls were laid out for extra room. Rising from the kitchen below, the delectable smell of freshly baked bread, hot pies, and roasted venison tempted trail-weary travelers. Elaborately crafted porticos, hedges, and flowering walkways led to a picnic grove lined by cottonwoods.

In this romantic spot, the pretty daughter of one of the station's landlords met the man of her dreams during a summer party. The friendly young southerner had an aristocratic bearing, which impressed the young woman and her family. Bound for the goldfields, he delayed the trip an extra day to spend more time with his new sweetheart. Despite their brief courtship, they fell in love and she promised to wait for him. After several months and the exchange of many letters, the young man returned to Glendale and the couple set a wedding date. To improve their prospects, the groom returned to the mines but sent word that he would be leaving from Cañon City with two friends in time for the ceremony. The bride's family prepared for an evening wedding followed by an elaborate feast.

On the appointed day, well-wishers flocked to Glendale House from all over Fremont County. Flowering garlands and bright ribbons hung from the balcony, and musicians entertained guests with lively tunes and soft ballads. As a crimson sunset spilled across the sky, several guests expressed concern over the groom's late arrival. The bride-to-be stationed herself on the porch, which provided a good view of the roadway. Dressed in her wedding gown, she waited for hours before dissolving in tears and retreating to her room. The next morning, several male guests formed a search party. A few miles down the road they found the young man, robbed and murdered by his companions.

The inconsolable young woman fell ill and died within the year. When the Denver & Rio Grande Railroad reached Leadville in 1880, traffic passing by the Glendale Station greatly diminished.

Still, travelers making the trip by horseback at night insisted that they saw a woman on the porch, her white satin gown glowing in the moonlight. The spectral figure may have been summoned by the click of the horseshoes upon the stone, since only riders on horseback could see her. Some even maintained they could hear the sound of her voice calling her lover's name and a pitiful sob just before she disappeared.

### ❧
# A Shadow behind the Wall

On February 8, 1886, the *Rocky Mountain Daily News* printed a bone-chilling tale told to an unnamed reporter by Charles Wharton, a man described only as "an old timer and gentleman of good judgment." A gruesome depiction of dark passion and murder, his account is difficult to prove or disprove more than a century later. Like all good ghost stories, however, it must have inspired speculation on those perennial dark and stormy Victorian nights.

"It was in the spring of 1881, just after the adjournment of the legislature with which I was connected, that I decided to move to Denver," Wharton began. "I sought for comfortable rooms within easy distance of the business portion. After several days' search, during which I examined pretty nearly every furnished apartment that was to let within the bounds I had set, I had about made up my mind to look further toward the suburbs."

Finally, a friend suggested a vacant suite of rooms on Champa Street. Almost hidden by trees and foliage, the modest-looking, two-story cottage stood back from the street, with a comfortable air that reminded him of a rural setting. When Wharton walked up the path and knocked on the door, a pleasant older woman greeted him. He noted that her face had deep lines of worry seemingly produced by something other than the simple ravages of time. The landlady showed him two pleasant rooms on the second floor connected by a door in the center of a partition wall. One of the long windows provided access to a small shaded veranda in front. After determining that the rent was reasonable, Wharton took the rooms and immediately went back to his hotel and arranged to have his luggage moved to the new quarters.

He returned to the suite about nine o'clock in the evening, made a fire in the grate, and sat down with a book to relax. "I had read for about two hours when I felt rather than saw that I was not alone," he said. "I looked up but could see nothing save the old fashioned pictures on the wall and the few articles of furniture in the room. The lamp had burned somewhat low and the blaze of the soft coal in the grate flickered in a fitful sort of way, casting peculiar shadows on the walls."

Wharton turned up the lamp, checked the fastenings on the doors and windows, and thoroughly searched both rooms. "I again sat down , resolved not to be again the victim of my imagination. I had not been seated very long before I again experienced the same sensation, accompanied by the soft rustle of a dress. I imagined I saw the outlines of a form *disappearing into the wall opposite.*"

Shaken by the experience, Wharton gave up reading and went to bed in the adjacent room, locking the door between the two apartments and leaving the lamplight low. After sleeping for an hour, he was awakened by the feel of a cold hand passing across his face. Upon awakening, he saw the dim outline of a human form, which gradually receded and passed through the door between the rooms. Trembling, he arose, turned up the lamp, and checked the doors, which were still fastened. After falling back into a fitful sleep, he awoke to a horrifying sight.

"Looking into the center room, which was illuminated by a ghostly light, I saw a fearful scene enacted," he told the reporter. "There were the figure of a man and woman, the latter dressed in a white robe, seemingly a white dress, evidently young and pretty, but for the steely, glassy eyes. The man was dragging her by the hair through the door from the other room. With a quick movement he thrust the woman to the floor and, with a glittering knife, cut her throat, almost severing the head from the body. Then ensued a series of shrieks and moans, followed by a crash as if the house had fallen into a mass."

Terrified and in a state of shock, Wharton lost consciousness. He awoke to bright sunshine the following morning happy to be alive. After summoning the courage to open the sitting room door he found everything in place. When he picked up the book he had been reading, however, he was shaken to find a drop of blood on the page. He packed up and moved out the same day.

"Soon the tenant of the other portion of the house moved away," Wharton continued. "It remained idle for nearly a year when it was torn down to make room for a handsome block. Feeling a curiosity about the old house, I went to look at it on the day it was demolished. Upon tearing down the outer wall, the workmen found a closet that appeared to have been closed up. In the bottom of the receptacle was found the skeleton of a woman."

After investigation, Wharton learned that some years earlier, a "notorious character" had lived in the house with his young and beautiful wife, about whom he had been inordinately jealous. One day both of them disappeared and were never heard from again. Since then, the house had changed tenants frequently. Apparently no one had ever stayed in Wharton's former room for more than one night.

## ❧
# The Suicide Chain

*T*he strange tale of the glamorous Josephine Stiles reads like a bad Victorian novel. Three husbands and a lover or two died for her sake, perhaps hoping to be reunited with the legendary beauty in the great beyond. Like a humorless *Midsummer Night's Dream*, the story of Josie's emotional entanglements provides a grim warning for those tempted to take romantic love too seriously.

Josephine Stiles left home in Pittsburgh when she was only twelve, wandering west as far as Butte, Montana. Her delicate features and mischievous dark eyes won scores of admirers, but Josie was a flirt and a hell-raiser by nature. When she arrived in Denver a few years later she became the toast of the town, winning several beauty contests along the way. Although the fickle Josie became "the belle of the West," her romantic relationships ended badly. Her first husband, Frank Blair, committed suicide soon after their separation. According to rumors, he wasn't the first man she pushed over the edge.

The seductress finally found happiness with second husband Billy Wardell, "whose principal claim to fame was that he owned all the lunch wagons in Denver, "according to a story in the *Denver Post*. A quarrel between the lovers may have inspired Wardell to leap from a viaduct into the Platte

River sometime in 1916. Although Josie married a third man, named Frank Stiles, she continued to mourn Wardell, surrounding herself with memorabilia from their relationship. On May 23, 1920, she told friends that she could hear Wardell's spirit calling to her, so she took poison to hasten their reunion. When Stiles returned home from work, he found her lying dead on their bed.

Stiles married again just four months later, but he still carried a torch for Josie. "For weeks he drank bottle after bottle of moonshine whiskey," complained his wife, Annie, in a *Post* interview. "He threatened to kill himself so he could go to Josie. … " In 1922, Stiles became the fourth casualty in the suicide chain when a guard found his body sprawled upon Josephine's grave at Crown Hill Cemetery. The coroner attributed his death to the combined effects of continued grieving and bad whiskey.

# 🎀
# The Uninvited Wedding Guest

With a giggle, the young bride-to-be dashed up the stairs before the wedding to hide from her future husband. As she reached the top of the carpeted staircase, she was startled by the reflection of a formally dressed gentleman in the glass door. He appeared to be passing behind her, but when she looked around, no one stood on the staircase. Perplexed, she peeked into the room behind the door, but still she saw no one. She later discovered that she'd caught a glimpse of the resident ghost of the Grant-Humphreys mansion, an uninvited guest who occasionally made an appearance to keep wedding parties on their toes.

Earlier that year, another bride had been primping for the wedding ceremony, checking the flowers in her hair, when she saw a man in coat and tails reflected in the mirror. To her amazement, he crossed the hallway, walked into her bedroom, and disappeared. A separate incident occurred a few weeks later, when the same elegant gentleman interrupted five bridesmaids while they dressed for a wedding. The terrified women dashed out of the room in their underwear, screaming that they had seen a ghost. Other jittery brides later reported seeing the intruder pass through the bedroom walls.

The benevolent denizen of Denver's Grant-Humphreys mansion may have been the ectoplasmic remains of Col. Albert Edmund Humphreys, an oil baron who purchased the neoclassical palace of former governor James Benton Grant in 1917. Grant built the impressive Capitol Hill home at 770 Pennsylvania Street for $40,000, but he encountered problems with his business and never quite finished the house. A forty-two-room palace with a theater in the basement, Grant-Humphreys sits high on a hill, just across from the governor's residence. One of Denver's most elegant mansions, the building features a semicircular portico that could have costarred in *Gone with the Wind.* An ocean of lawn peppered with large hardwood trees skirts the main entrance.

Albert Humphreys purchased the mansion from Grant's widow. A southern gentleman who probably felt quite at home in the Tara-like setting, Humphreys made few alterations other than adding a ten-car garage with gas pumps and a car wash to service his stable of vehicular thoroughbreds. The mansion stayed in the family until 1976, when the colonel's oldest son, Ira E., donated the property to the Colorado State Historical Society for a house museum. Haunted or not, Grant-Humphreys became a popular site for formal events, particularly weddings.

At first glance, Colonel Humphreys hardly seems the kind of man who would frighten young women out of their underwear. Born in Sissonville, West Virginia, in 1860, Humphreys received a teacher's certificate from Marshall College before he turned sixteen. While working on a degree at Northwestern University in Illinois, he helped with his father's lumber business. He made and lost both timber and mining fortunes before he struck it rich in the oil fields of Oklahoma and Texas. After he married Alice Boyd in 1887, the couple lived in Duluth, Minnesota, and moved to Colorado nine years later.

One of Denver's most generous philanthropists, Humphreys reportedly gave away nearly a million dollars during his lifetime and established Colorado's first foundation in 1922. Highly religious, he assisted missionary enterprises of the Central Christian Church and the Sunshine mission in Colorado. Unfortunately, he became involved with the Teapot Dome Scandal during the 1920s, when the Department of the Interior was charged with leasing prime oilfields near Teapot Dome, Wyoming, to wealthy investors without competitive bidding. Many of Humphreys's cronies were subject to a congressional investigation, and Humphreys himself was subpoenaed to testify in the bribery trial of the secretary of the interior. In December 1926, Humphreys suffered a bout with double pneumonia, forcing postponement of the trial until he could recover. He was being treated for a "nervous disorder" through Colorado General Hospital in May 1927 when a particularly grisly incident ended his life at age sixty-six.

The colonel appeared to be in good spirits that Sunday afternoon as he prepared to visit his summer retreat, the End of the Road Ranch at Wagon Wheel gap, just east of Creede. After dinner he went upstairs, presumably to pack.

Newspaper reports speculated that Humphreys had been examining one of his shotguns when it discharged, tearing away part of his lower jaw and throat. His male nurse, J. H. Schasky, ran upstairs to investigate the noise and immediately summoned the family. Unable to speak and facing permanent disfigurement even if he survived, Humphreys scribbled a note: "Please give me chloroform and let me die." Somehow the gravely injured man walked to the stairs (some witnesses said that he tried to throw himself down the staircase) before the ambulance took him away to Mercy Hospital. The colonel wrote two more notes, both begging for death, before he finally expired at 6:45 P.M., three hours after the shooting. Rumors circulated that Humphreys had committed suicide or, even worse, had been the victim of foul play. Fellow hunters maintained that an experienced marksman like Colonel Humphreys would never accidentally shoot himself in the face while cleaning a gun. To add to the mystery, Humphreys's nurse, Schasky, disappeared soon after the shooting. Some whispered that the nurse had been an assassin, hired to make sure that the colonel would never testify. Or perhaps Humphreys found himself in a moral dilemma and saw suicide as the only way out. In any event, the official verdict was accidental death.

Stories about the house being haunted came to the attention of the media in the early 1980s, a few years after the family donated the property to the historical society. On Halloween night in 1984, radio station KNUS featured a remote broadcast from the mansion with nationally known psychic Yvonne Ciardullo and David Brose, the museum's director. The psychic identified not one, but three ghosts: Colonel Humphreys, an unknown little girl, and a Latino man who had died on the property without receiving last rites. Ciardullo later reported that "There was a gentleman there, waiting to go to the light," and that she guided him in the proper direction. The *Rocky Mountain News* interviewed the psychic three years later: "Ciardullo says many people have trouble believing, as she does, in the nonphysical entities she calls ghosts. 'But that's OK,' she says. 'Everyone has their own reality. And I have mine.'"

Since the "exorcism," the museum has been quiet except for an occasional noisy party and mysterious flashing lights reported by neighbors. Although some Grant-Humphreys personnel bristle at the implication that their beloved property ever had a ghost, an occasional visitor has felt a "presence" in the theater downstairs. The colonel could be watching some invisible performance on the stage, or perhaps he's just waiting for another Halloween Haunted House tour.

# Bibliography

## Books

Allen, Alexandra. *Travelling Ladies, Victorian Adventuresses.* London: Jupiter Books, 1980.

Arps, Louisa Ward. *Denver in Slices.* Athens, Ohio: Swallow Press Books, Ohio University Press, 1959.

Bancroft, Caroline. *Silver Queen, the Fabulous Story of Baby Doe Tabor.* Boulder, Colo.: Johnson Printing, 1955.

Becker, Cynthia S. and David. P. Smith. *Chipeta, Queen of the Utes.* Montrose, Colo.: Western Reflections Publishing, 2003.

Bird, Isabella. *A Lady's Life in the Rocky Mountains.* Norman: University of Oklahoma Press, 1960.

Birmingham, Stephen. *The Grande Dames, Part Six, A Woman of Mystery.* New York: Simon and Schuster, 1982.

Blackwelder, Bernice. *Great Westerner, the Story of Kit Carson.* Caldwell, Idaho: Caxton Printers, 1962.

Bundles, A'Lelia. *On Her Own Ground, The Life and Times of Madam C. J. Walker.* New York: Scribner Publishing, 2001.

Byers, William N. *History of Colorado.* Chicago: Century Publishing and Engraving, 1901.

Carson, Christopher. *Kit Carson's Autobiography.* Edited by Milo Milton Quaife. Lincoln: University of Nebraska Press, 1966.

Carter, Harvey Lewis. *"Dear Old Kit" The Historical Christopher Carson.* Norman: University of Oklahoma Press, 1968.

DeArment, Robert K. *Knights of the Green Cloth: the Saga of Frontier Gamblers.* Norman: University of Oklahoma Press, 1982.

Dier, Caroline Lawrence. *The Lady of the Gardens, Mary Elitch Long.* Hollywood, Calif.: Hollycrofters, 1932.

Dodds, Joanne West. *What's a Nice Girl Like You Doing in a Place Like This?* Pueblo, CO: Focal Plain, 1996.

Evalyn Walsh McClean. *Father Struck It Rich.* Ouray, Colo.: Bear Creek Publishing, 1981.

Fowler, Gene, *Timberline: Denver—the Rip Roaring Years:* Comstock Editions, Inc., 1977.

Goodstein, Phil. *The Ghosts of Denver: Capitol Hill.* Denver: New Social Publications, 1996.

Goodstein, Phil. *The Seamy Side of Denver.* Denver: New Social Publications, 1993.

Hull, Betty Lynne. *Denver's Elitch Gardens, Spinning a Century of Dreams.* Boulder Colo.: Johnson Books, 2003.

Iversen, Kristen. *Molly Brown, Unraveling the Myth.* Boulder, Colo.: Johnson Printing, 1999.

Kreck, Dick. *Murder at the Brown Palace.* Golden, Colo.: Fulcrum Publishing, 2003.

Lee, Mabel Barbee. *Cripple Creek Days.* Garden City, N.Y.: Doubleday & Co., 1958.

Leonard, Stephen J. and Thomas J. Noel. *Denver, Mining Camp to Metropolis.* Boulder, Colo.:University Press of Colorado, 1990.

Levine, Brian. *Cripple Creek Gold: A Centennial History of the Cripple Creek District.* Lake Grove, Ore: The Depot, 1988.

Luchetti, Cathy. *I Do! Courtship, Love and Marriage on the American Frontier.* New York: Crown Trade Paperbacks, 1996.

Martin, MaryJoy. *Twilight Dwellers, Ghosts, Ghouls and Goblins of Colorado.* Boulder, Colo.: Pruitt Publishing, 1955.

Martin, Ralph G. *Golda Meir, the Romantic Years.* New York: Charles Scribner's Sons, 1988.

Meir, Golda. *My Life.* New York: G.P. Putnam's Sons, 1975.

Meir, Menachem. *My Mother, Golda Meir.* New York: Arbor House, 1983.

Noel, Thomas J. *Denver, Rocky Mountain Gold.* Tulsa, Okla.: Continental Heritage Press, 1980.

Noel, Thomas J., Stephen J. Leonard, and Kevin E. Rucker. *Colorado Givers, A History of Philanthropic Heroes.* Niwot, Colo.: University Press of Colorado, 1998.

Norman, Cathleen M. and Thomas J. Noel. *A Pikes Peak Partnership, the Penroses, the Tutts and El Pomar.* Niwot, Colo.: University Press of Colorado, 2001.

Padgett, Carol. *Keeping Hearth and Home in Old Colorado.* Birmingham, Ala.: Menasha Ridge Press, 2002.

Panati, Charles. *Extraordinary Origins of Everyday Things.* New York: Harper & Row, 1987.

Parkhill, Forbes. *Donna Madixxa Goes West.* Boulder Colo.: Pruett Press, 1968.

Parkhill, Forbes. *The Wildest of the West.* Denver: Sage Books, 1957.

Peiss, Kathy. *The Making of America's Beauty Culture.* New York: Metropolitan Books, Henry Holt & Co., 1998.

Perkin, Robert L. *The First Hundred Years; An Informal History of Denver and the Rocky Mountain News.* Garden City, N.Y.: Doubleday, 1959.

Pettem, Sylvia. *Separate Lives, the Story of Mary Rippon.* Longmont, Colo.: The Book Lode, 1999.

Plante, Ellen M. *Women at Home in Victorian America, A Social History.* New York: Facts on File, 1997.

Preiss, Kathy. *Beauty in a Jar.* New York: Metropolitan Books, Henry Holt and Co., 1998.

Reed, Verner Z. *Tales of the Sun-Land.* New York: Continental Publishing Co., 1897.

Rockwell, Wilson. *The Utes, A Forgotten People.* Ouray, Colo.: Western Reflections, 1998.

Sanford, Mollie Dorsey. *Mollie, the Journal of Mollie Dorsey Sanford.* Lincoln: University of Nebraska Press, 1959.

Seagraves, Anne. *Soiled Doves, Prostitution in the Early West.* Hayden, Idaho: Wesanne Publications, 1994.

Secrest, Clark. *Hell's Bells, Prostitution and Crime in Early Denver.* Rev. ed. Niwot, Colo.: University of Colorado Press, 2002.

Simmons, Marc. *Kit Carson and His Three Wives.* Albuquerque: University of New Mexico Press, 2003.

Smiley, Jerome C. *A History of Denver.* Evansville, Ind.:, The Times-Sun Publishing Co., 1901.

Smith, Duane A. *Horace Tabor, His Life and the Legend.* Niwot, Colo.: University Press of Colorado, 1989.

Smith, P. David. *Ouray, Chief of the Utes.* Ouray, Colo.: Wayfinder Press, 1986.

Sprague, Marshall. *Money Mountain, the Story of Cripple Creek Gold.* Lincoln: University of Nebraska Press,1953.

Stella M. Drumm, ed. *Down the Santa Fe Trail and into Mexico, The Diary of Susan Shelby Magoffin, 1846–1847.* New Haven, Conn.: Yale University Press, 1962.

Ubbelohde, Carl, Maxine Benson, and Duane A. Smith. *A Colorado History.* Boulder, Colo: Pruett Publishing, 1976.

Whitacre, Christine. *Molly Brown, Denver's Unsinkable Lady.* Denver: Historic Denver, 1984.

Willison, George F. *Here They Dug the Gold.* New York: Bretano's, 1931.

Zamonski, Stanley W. and Teddy Keller. *The Fifty-Niners,* Denver: Stanz-Harp, 1957.

## Magazines, Journals, and Newspapers

*Cañon City Daily Record*
*Canyon City Avalanche*
*Central City Call-Register*
*Christian Advocate*
*Colorado Gambler*
*Colorado Heritage*
*Colorado Homes and Lifestyles*
*Colorado Prospector*
*Cycling West*
*The Denver (Evening) Post*
*The Denver Republican*
*The Denver Times*
*Denver Westerners Roundup*
*Engineering and Mining Journal*
*Golden Transcript*
*Grand Junction Sentinel*
*Historic Denver News*
*Leadville Chronicle*
*Overland News*
*Pueblo Chieftain*
*Rocky Mountain Herald*
*Rocky Mountain News*

## Manuscripts and Documents

Alberta Iliff Shattuck, the Denver Fortnightly Club. "Singer Comes to Colorado." Ira J. Taylor Library, Iliff School of Theology: February 17, 1976.

Sanford, Mollie. Diary of Mollie Dorsey Sanford, 1895–1900. Littleton History Museum

Benjamin Draper Colorado Theater Collection 1859–1967. Denver
    Public Library Western History & Genealogy.
Nichols, Dean G., Pioneer Theaters of Denver, Colorado. Denver
    Public Library Western History and Genealogy.

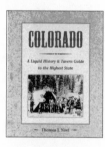